THE DEVOTIONAL EXPERIENCE
IN THE POETRY OF
JOHN MILTON

THE DEVOTIONAL EXPERIENCE IN THE POETRY OF JOHN MILTON

Michael Ernest Travers

Studies in Art and Religious Interpretation
Volume 10

The Edwin Mellen Press
Lewiston/Queenston

Library of Congress Cataloging-in-Publication Data

Travers, Michael Ernest.
The devotional experience in the poetry of John Milton.

(Studies in art and religious interpretation ; v. 10)
Bibliography: p.
Includes index.
1. Milton, John, 1608-1674--Criticism and
interpretation. 2. Devotional literature, English--
History and criticism. 3. Christian poetry, English--
History and criticism. I. Title. II. Series.
PR3592.D45T7   1987   821.'4   87-28128
ISBN 0-88946-562-2

This is volume 10 in the continuing series
Studies in Art and Religious Interpretation
ISBN 0-88946-562-2
SARI Series ISBN 0-88946-956-3

The Edwin Mellen Press
Box 450
Lewiston, New York
USA 14092

The Edwin Mellen Press
Box 67
Queenston, Ontario
L0S 1L0 CANADA

Printed in the United States of America

DEDICATION

"For Barbara,
Stephen and
Elizabeth"

Acknowledgements

No book was ever researched, written, revised and published by a single person. Every author owes a debt to colleagues, typists, and an editor; many owe thanks to a foundation or institution for financial assistance. I acknowledge my debts gratefully.

I am grateful to Donald Rosenberg, Philip McGuire, Roger Meiners and Douglas Peterson, all of Michigan State University, for their substantive scholarly advice and their constant vigilance throughout the drafting of the present work. I owe thanks to Pat Heerspink and Ginger Sweat, both of whom typed and retyped early drafts of the manuscript under pressure of deadlines. I could not have prepared this manuscript for the publisher had it not been for a most generous grant from Liberty University, under the direction of Russell Fitzgerald, Vice President for Academic Affairs at that institution; I am grateful for this financial assistance. I thank Marguerite Rupnow of Lewiston Business Services, whose expertise and knowledge of the details of manuscript preparation made possible the publication of this book on time. I am grateful for the support and guidance of Herbert Richardson, my editor. Without the extensive and varied contributions of these people, this book could not have been published.

My greatest debt is given in the dedication. Thank you all.

TABLE OF CONTENTS

Introduction

As a result of Milton's conviction that each person is responsible for taking God into account in his life, the reader of Milton's works is aware of two general subjects.[1] In The Christian Poet in "Paradise Lost", William G. Riggs identifies these two subjects as "God's dealings with man and man's dealings with God."[2] Although Riggs' statement is limited to Paradise Lost in particular, it applies to Milton's poetry in general: Milton justifies God's ways to man and shows man how to approach God. His major poems are theodicies in that they attempt to present God's actions in human lives in comprehensible terms; they are devotions in that they attempt to show men how to respond to God and His actions in their lives. I wish to examine one of these two subjects, the experience of man's devotion to God, in Milton's poetic theories and his major poetry from 1629 to 1671. I wish to argue that Milton's own devotion to God is an active expression of his love for God and that he communicates this devotion in his view of poetry and in the experience of the speakers and characters in his poems.

Milton was certainly not the only writer of religious poetry in seventeenth century England; indeed, the seventeenth century provided some of the best devotional poetry in all of English literature. One of the most striking characteristics of devotional poetry of the day was its breadth. No one religious poet dominated the writing of devotional poetry; no one religious credo prescribed the forms that devotion was to take in poetry. Roman Catholics, such as Robert Southwell and Richard Crashaw, wrote great "meditative" poetry after the Ignatian model which Louis L. Martz analyzes so thoroughly in The Poetry of Meditation (1954). Anglicans, such as John Donne and George Herbert, wrote devotional poetry and also many sermons that challenged the reader to meditate on religious subjects[3] both informally and formally.[4] And Puritans, such as John Milton and Edward Taylor (in Massachusetts) wrote a type of poetry that was generally devotional in tone. Nor does this list exhaust the roll-call of seventeenth century devotional poets; Quarles, Vaughan and Traherne are other religious poets of the century whose poetry, in addition to that of those already mentioned, has come to be regarded as important devotional literature. The seventeenth century, then, produced religious poetry of great quality and quantity.

There were, however, at least two important "traditions" of devotional poetry in Milton's England. Just as the Reformers, beginning in 1517 with Martin Luther's "Ninety Five Theses" had reacted against the Roman Catholic church, so too the Roman Catholic church reacted against the Protestants in 1534 with the Counter Reformation establishment of the Order of the Jesuits by Ignatius Loyola. The sixteenth-century split in the church, underscored in England by Henry VIII's decision to divorce Catherine of Aragon and by Elizabeth I's efforts to strengthen and defend the Church of England, led inevitably to two types of devotion, the Roman Catholic and Reformed. The study of these methods of devotion, and the poetry that developed from them, is a complex one. Louis L. Martz examines the Roman Catholic Ignatian and Salesian[5] models of meditation of the Counter Reformation in The Poetry of Meditation. Barbara K. Lewalski analyzes the Reformed mode of devotion in her book, Protestant Poetics and the Seventeenth Century Religious Lyric (1979). She identifies the characteristics of the Protestant devotion -- what she calls "the Protestant paradigm" (p. 10) -- and analyzes the poetry of Donne, Herbert, Vaughan, Traherne and Taylor in that light. Although it is not possible to prove that Milton borrowed exclusively from one of these two traditions, nevertheless he did not write in an intellectual vacuum, unaware of the major devotional traditions of his day. Therefore, let me examine briefly the general characteristics of Ignatian and Protestant devotion -- and the Augustinian perception of devotion which lies behind them.

In The Poetry of Meditation, Louis L. Martz claims that Roman Catholic Ignatian methods of meditation provided the "method" for seventeenth century English religious literature:

> But fundamentally, I shall argue, the Counter Reformation penetrated to English literature through methods of religious meditation that lay at the heart of the century's spiritual life and provided a radiant center for religious literature of every kind.[6]

From his study of Ignatian and Salesian handbooks of meditation, Martz establishes that a tripartite structure is characteristic of the meditative poetry of the sixteenth and seventeenth centuries. According to this model, the first step in a meditative poem is "composition, seeing the spot" -- the writer focuses on the subject at hand or on the object of devotion. Second comes the "understanding," or analysis, of those affections that would best move the will to appropriate meditation. The third step is the "colloquy," in which the affections are "stirred up" and the will is brought into devotion, or love, for the object at hand (p. 40). The value of this tripartite Ignatian structure in understanding meditative poetry is its application to brief, self-contained lyrics that introduce, develop, and conclude a meditation.[7] Martz's commentary is particularly useful in the analysis of the early seventeenth century devotional lyrics of Donne, Herbert and Vaughan. (It must be granted that Martz applies his understanding of meditation to Paradise Regained in The Paradise Within.) His study alone, however, does not explain Milton's expression of devotion adequately, especially in the longer poems.

It would of course be natural for Milton to turn to Protestant, even Puritan, types of devotion rather than Roman Catholic meditations as models for his own writing. In Protestant Poetics and the Seventeenth-Century Religious Lyric, Barbara Lewalski argues that seventeenth century Protestant devotions concentrate more on St. Paul's theology than on Ignatian meditative structures. She states:

The Pauline terms -- election, calling, justification, adoption, sanctification, glorification -- mark the important stages (some of them concomitant rather than sequential) in the spiritual life of any Protestant Christian, who was urged by dozens of manuals to seek constantly for the evidence of those stages in his own life.

p. 16

Lewalski cites three significant distinctions between Protestant and Roman Catholic meditation. First, the Protestant poet returns directly to the Bible for the subjects of his devotion; this is in keeping with the Reformers' position of sola scriptura -- the Bible alone as the rule of faith and practice.[8] Milton's three major poems, for instance, are based on biblical narratives.

Second, the Protestant meditation does not follow a strict structure; its "stages" can be "concomitant" as well as sequential. Hence, Protestant devotion has no single, universally recognized structure to identify it. In the Protestant meditative tradition, therefore, Milton was able to find the flexibility which he needed in order to write long narrative poems in which the characters experience devotion in a variety of ways.

Lewalski's third point is that the Protestant meditator examines his own life for evidence of God's grace in his election, calling, justification, adoption, sanctification and glorification. The Protestant meditator does not approach God on the basis of his meditation; rather, he rehearses his own experience of God's grace. Lewalski elaborates on the difference between Ignatian and Protestant devotion:

The manner of application to the self in Protestant meditation also distinguishes it from Ignatian or Salesian meditation. In these continental kinds, the meditator typically seeks to apply himself to the subscene vividly, as if it were taking place in his presence, analyzes the subject, and stirs up emotions appropriate to the scene or event or personal spiritual condition. The typical Protestant procedure is very nearly the reverse: instead of the application of the self to the subject, it calls for the application of the subject to the self -- indeed for the subject's location in the self . . .

pp. 149 -150

In Protestant devotional poetry, the meditator does not actively stir his emotions up to worship the subject (God); rather, Protestant devotion is characterized by a search on the part of the meditator for the already-existing evidences in his own experience of the actions of God. Milton's devotion is close to this Protestant paradigm.

Behind both the Roman Catholic and Reformed traditions of meditation is St. Augustine's commentary on the subject of devotion, or worship. Milton was familiar with Augustine's City of God[9] and surely must have been aware of his comments on devotion to God. Roger Hazelton's 1955 article, "The Devotional Life," makes a far-reaching claim regarding the influence of Augustine on western modes of worship and devotion:

. . . he [Augustine] likewise marked the channels of Christian devotion, from his time to our own. His stamp upon the prayer-ways of the Christian West, both Catholic and Protestant, has been no less deep and enduring than his monumental theological influence. The great themes which recur in Christian worship, the images and metaphors by which the devotional spirit is perennially nourished, the very words and phrases by which Christians in public or in private recall themselves to God -- these are still in large part indubitably Augustinian.[10]

Hazelton attributes the major themes, images and metaphors of Christian devotion in both its Roman Catholic and Protestant forms to St. Augustine.

Barbara Lewalski agrees that Augustine's comments on devotion were important and that both Roman Catholics and Protestants regarded him "as a primary point of reference" in the subject (p. 215). Louis Martz introduces The Paradise Within with a preface that argues for the centrality of Augustine's teachings on worship in seventeenth century meditative poetry.

Of particular importance in Martz's discussion is his identification of the "paradise within" and the image of God in man. He states:

> . . . the image of God is manifested not in the mere passive possession of certain qualities but in the action, the power to use reason for its proper ends. [11]

The important point for this discussion is the idea that the image of God is active, not passive. Milton agrees with this idea throughout his poetry. His characters express their love for God actively: Adam and Eve repent of their sin; the Son does not succumb to the temptations in the wilderness; and Samson defeats the Philistines by his own death.

It would be impossible to claim that Milton restricts his perception of devotion to the Ignatian, Reformed or Augustinian method of devotion. Nor can we argue that he moves consistently toward one of these models of devotion in his poetry. He is closer in his later poetry to Augustinian or Reformed devotion than he is to the Ignatian structure of meditation, but I do not wish to assert that he designs his poems on any specific model of devotion. Rather, Milton is original in his depiction of devotion -- as he is in his works in general. He integrates a vast range of influences into his own unique work. His poetry is his own, made in his own image, so to speak, not a casual collection of others' materials. His contribution to devotional literature is this union of devotion and narrative and dramatic poetry. In Paradise Lost, Paradise Regained, and Samson Agonistes in particular, he expresses devotion within the narrative development itself. The integration of devotion with narration allows him to develop devotion as an active, not a passive, experience; and it allows devotion to be an expression of character. This is Milton's genius in devotional literature: devotion is the active and inevitable articulation of a character's love for God as he experiences it in the actual development of narrative events. Fortunately, Milton provides us with a clear statement outside of his poetry of his perspective of devotion and love for God in The Christian Doctrine.

Because The Christian Doctrine is the only systematic statement of Milton's theology, it is important for us to understand what he says there about devotion. He considers the subject of devotion in Book Two of The Christian Doctrine under the heading of the worship of God. He distinguishes the worship of God in Book Two from the knowledge of God in Book One. Because he separates worship from the knowledge of God proper, he presents worship (with devotion included as a type of worship) as less a doctrine than an "affection." Specifically, devotion is the affection of love toward God, a love which is directed properly toward God alone (CE, XVIII, p. 3). Milton further restricts the subject of devotion by placing it in the category of "internal," as opposed to "external," worship. For Milton, external worship has to do with the public and outward forms of worship (CE, XVIII, p. 51 and 53); "internal worship," on the other hand, "consists mainly in the acknowledgment of the one true God, and in the cultivation of devout affections toward him" (CE, XVIII, p. 51). Devotion is an individual's inner attitude toward God which he expresses in the "cultivation," or active development, of certain "devout affections" for Him.

Milton defines this devotional love as "that by which we prefer him [God] above all other objects of affection, and desire his glory" (CE, XVII, pp. 51 and 53). As Milton's references to Deuteronomy 6:5 and Matthew 22:37 indicate, we are to love God "with all [our] soul[s], and with all [our] might." God is to be the object of our hearts' love, and that even at the expense of our love for the things of this world. Indeed, the love of the world is hatred of God, as Milton makes clear. He cites a number of scriptural texts in support of this argument, especially James 4:4 in which James asks, "Know ye not that the friendship of the world is enmity with

God? whoever therefore will be a friend of the world is the enemy of God."[12] The kind of love that Milton calls devotion is a type of love that is a free, conscious act of the will which chooses God over the things of this world.

The deliberate choice of God is a necessary part of devotional love for Milton. Love must come from a free will, else it is not proper devotion at all. In The Christian Doctrine Milton identifies seven different ways that a person may choose to express his devotion to God. They are what he calls "devout affections": trust, hope, gratitude, fear, humility, patience, and obedience (CE, XVII, p. 51). He defines each one specifically in The Christian Doctrine; it is these affections which Milton uses to develop an appropriate devotional love for God in the lives of the characters of his poems.

In order to understand Milton's depiction of the experience of devotion, we shall examine in Chapter One his statement regarding poetry and the nature of the poetic talent that are relevant to devotion. We will also locate his comments within his theology, specifically his theory that God's general grace is the foundation for poetry. It will be necessary, therefore, to examine briefly Milton's statement regarding the nature and limits of divine inspiration in poetry. Finally, we will outline Milton's definitions of the seven devout affections. These issues in poetic theory provide the material for Chapter One and form the theoretical foundations for the later studies of devotion in Milton's poetry in subsequent chapters.

In Chapter Two, we shall examine the "Nativity Ode," "The Passion," and "Lycidas" inasmuch as they demonstrate Milton beginning to develop devotion in his poetry. These poems, written between 1629 and 1637, were composed during a period of intense preparation on Milton's part for his career as a poet. He was searching for the "right" way to use his God-given talent of writing.[13] These were the years preceding the Civil War; they were private years for Milton, among his last until the Restoration.

During the 1630's, Milton wrote many important poems, at least three of which begin to develop the experience of devotion.

Chapter Three deals with Paradise Lost. It is obviously impossible in one chapter to conduct a sustained analysis of the poem in its entirety. The poem is too long and complex to allow that kind of comprehensive treatment. Therefore, we shall examine selected passages that develop the experience of love toward God most directly. These passages are primarily the speeches of Adam and Eve at significant points in the narrative, though the Son's speeches provide an important counterpoint to the devotion which Adam and Eve experience -- especially after the fall. Indeed, a division of Paradise Lost into its prelapsarian and postlapsarian sections provides an effective and appropriate perspective of the experience of devotion in the lives of Adam and Eve, the central characters in the poem.

In Chapter Four we shall analyze the development of devotion in the life of the Son of God in Paradise Regained. Through the temptations in the wilderness, the Son learns how to express his love for God. Milton emphasizes the humanity of his protagonist in Paradise Regained, even when he identifies him as "the Son of God" (thirty-nine times), "Savior" (twenty-one times), "Messiah" (seven times), and "Jesus" (six times).[14] Milton consistently stresses the Son's need to prove himself worthy to redeem men from their sins throughout the poem. The point is that Milton clearly wishes to emphasize the humanity of his protagonist so that he can develop in understanding and emotion in the poem.

The final chapter examines Samson Agonistes with reference to the development of proper devotion in the experience of Samson himself. Samson is particularly appropriate as a model of devotion for two reasons. First, he is an Old Testament saint, whose life demonstrates that Milton thought of devotion as an experience available to all men. Second, Samson has no one to turn to but God: the Hebrew leaders desert him and Dalila betrays him; Manoa does not understand him and Harapha taunts him. God alone appreciates the depth of his discouragement. In the character of Samson, Milton presents devotion in its most practical and integrated form.

This is the plan of the study. It presumes, first, that Milton wrote Paradise Lost between 1655 and 1663 for publication in 1667, and then wrote Paradise Regained and Samson Agonistes for 1671 publication. Though he had plans for the final two poems early in his career, he did not write the poems as we now have them until late in life.[15] Second, the approach to the poems presumes that, because Milton was always conscious of his divine call as a poet,[16] he was developing the theology of The Christian Doctrine simultaneously with the writing of his major poems;[17] therefore, Milton's doctrine of general grace as we have it in The Christian Doctrine is important to an understanding of his later poetry. Finally, I rely on the traditional chronology in order to allow the development of devotion in Milton's works.

Notes
Introduction

[1]John Milton, The Works of John Milton, Edited by Frank Allen Patterson (New York: Columbia University Press, 1931-42), XIV, p. 5. All references throughout the book to The Christian Doctrine are made to the Columbia Edition and are cited in the text as CE

[2]William G. Riggs, The Christian Poet in "Paradise Lost" (Berkeley: University of California Press, 1972), p. 2. All subsequent references to this work will be cited in the text.

[3]Barbara Lewalski, Protestant Poetics and the Seventeenth Century Religious Lyric (Princeton: Princeton University Press, 1979), p. 150.

[4]Lewalski, p. 151.

[5]Lewalski, p. 149. All subsequent reference to this work will be cited in the text of the book.

[6]Louis L. Martz, The Poetry of Meditation (New Haven: Yale University Press, 1954), p. 10. All subsequent references to this work will be cited in the text of the book.

[7]Martz, p. 40 and compare Edward Dawson, in "The Practical Method of Meditation," The Meditative Poem (New York: New York University Press, 1963), p. 12.

[8]Isabel Rivers, Classical and Christian Ideas in English Renaissance Poetry (Boston: George Allen and Unwin, 1979), pp. 101-02. Also CE, XIV, p. 15. All subsequent references to Rivers will be cited in the text of the book.

[9]James Holly Hanford, A Milton Handbook 4th ed. (New York: Appleton-Century-Crofts, 1954), p. 246. Compare Denis Saurat, Milton: Man and Thinker (New York: The Dial Press, Inc., 1925), p. 273. All subsequent references to Hanford will be cited in the text of the book.

[10]Roger Hazelton, "The Devotional Life," in A Companion to the Study of St. Augustine, ed. Roy Battenhouse (New York: Oxford University Press, 1969), p. 398. All subsequent references to this work will be cited in the text of the book.

[11]Louis L. Martz, The Paradise Within (New Haven: Yale University Press, 1964), pp. 200 and xiv. All subsequent references to this work will be cited in the text of the book.

[12]All references to the Bible are taken from the King James Version.

[13]John Spencer Hill, John Milton: Poet, Priest and Prophet (Totowa, New Jersey: Rowman and Littlefield, 1979), pp. 52-53. All subsequent references to this work will be cited in the text of the book.

[14]Martz, The Paradise Within, p. 180.

[15]Hanford, pp. 190-91; 269.

[16]John Milton, "The Reason of Church Government Urged Against Prelaty," John Milton: Complete Poems and Major Prose, Edited by Merritt Y. Hughes (New York: The Odyssey Press, 1957), pp. 666-68. All subsequent references to this work will be cited in the text of the book.

[17]Arthur Sewell, A Study of Milton's Christian Doctrine (Folcroft, PA: Archon Books, 1967), pp. 33 and 123. All subsequent references to this work will be cited in the text of the book.

CHAPTER ONE
Poetic Theories

Blest pair of Sirens, pledges of Heav'n's joy,
Sphere-born harmonious Sisters, Voices and Verse,
Wed your divine sounds, and mixt power employ
Dead things with inbreath'd sense able to pierce,
And to our high-rais'd fantasy present
That undisturbed Song of pure concent,
Aye sung before the sapphire-color'd throne
To him that sits thereon,
With Saintly shout and solemn Jubilee,
Where the bright Seraphim in burning row
Their loud uplifted Angel-trumpets blow,
And the Cherubic host in thousand choirs
Touch their immortal Harps of golden wires,
With those just Spirits that wear victorious Palms,
Hymns devout and holy Psalms
Singing everlastingly;
That we on Earth with undiscording voice
May rightly answer that melodious noise;
As once we did, till disproportion'd sin
Jarr'd against nature's chime, and with harsh din
Broke the fair music that all creatures made
To their great Lord, whose love their motion sway'd
In perfect Diapason, whilst they stood
In first obedience and their state of good.
O may we soon again renew that Song,
And keep in tune with Heav'n, till God ere long

To his celestial consort us unite,
To live with him, and sing in endless morn of light.[1]

I have quoted "At a Solemn Music" (1633) in its entirety, not to discuss Milton's views of music, but to suggest his perspective on the arts in general and on poetry in particular. Milton believes the orthodox Christian teaching that God created us originally in a "state of good" and that, in that good state, we were in harmony, or "perfect Diapason" as he calls it here, with the Creator. That is to say, there was no "discord," or lack of understanding between the Creator and man. However, man fell into sin and therefore out of harmony with God. Milton describes sin in this poem as "disproportioned" and "against" nature; sin "broke the fair music that all creatures made / To their great Lord." Because of his sin, man lost a full understanding of God's ways in his life; this is the reason that Milton feels the need to "justify the ways of God to men" in Paradise Lost.

How then can fallen man communicate with God? Milton believes that the art of poetry (as well as music[2]) can be an act of devotion to God, even after the fall:

O May we soon again renew that Song
And keep in tune with Heav'n, til God ere long
To his celestial consort us unite,
To live with him, and sing in endless morn of light.

The ultimate purpose of music and poetry is eschatological: it is praise to God when we are in heaven. But music and poetry composed on this earth even before that final day when we are all "united" in heaven can celebrate and worship God. This is Milton's reason for writing poetry -- to express his personal love to God. And, as we have seen in his definition of devotion in The Christian Doctrine, love for God is devotion. Milton's poetry expresses his own devotion to God.

Milton echoes the same thought about learning in general in Of Education, written in 1644:

> The end of learning is to repair the ruins of our first parents by regaining to know God aright, and out of that knowledge to love him . . .
>
> p. 631

Milton's thoughts about the nature of poetry (because it is one method of teaching[3]) are inextricably related to his orthodox thinking about the creation of man, his fall, and the manner in which fallen man communicates with God. We are to come to "know God aright" again; this is accomplished in large part in Milton's view by God's grace.

Milton's doctrine of divine grace is important to his poetic theories, particularly insofar as it relates to his thinking regarding the worship of God in poetry. While Milton believes that poetry is a means of worshiping God, he does not think that fallen man can express devotion to God without God's first extending grace to him.[4] This is prevenient grace. Only God, in His work of "regeneration," can "create afresh, as it were, the inward man" and restore him to future good works:

> Regeneration is that change operated by the Word and the Spirit, whereby the old man being destroyed, the inward man is regenerated by God after his own image, in all the faculties of his mind, insomuch that he becomes as it were a new creature, and the whole man is sanctified both in body and soul, for the service of God, and the performance of good works.
>
> CE, XV, p. 367

In order for any of man's works, including his expressions of love in poetry, to be acceptable to God in Milton's view, man must be "regenerated" so that he is "sanctified both in body and soul, for the service of God."

Without this divine sanctification in a fallen man's life, his poetry is unacceptable to God as an expression of love. Man must become a "new creature" in Milton's view before his "good works" can serve God. God makes a "new creature" by His grace.

Milton holds to a doctrine of general grace that has to do with all of God's activities in men's lives. For Milton, God gives grace to man in two particular ways. The first evidence of God's grace in man's life is His universal offer of salvation. God gives sufficient grace to all men for their salvation through His grace:

> . . . he [God] undoubtedly gives grace to all, if not in equal measure, at least sufficient for attaining knowledge of the truth and final salvation.
>
> CE, XIV, p. 147

The Calvinistic doctrine that God "reprobates" some men to hell and "elects" others to heaven is anathema to Milton.[5] He teaches rather that God offers enough grace to all men for their salvation; salvation is the making of a new creature fit for God's service. Beyond that saving grace, however, God provides a second evidence of His grace: He gives more grace to certain men to serve Him more fully than others. Milton notes that God's grace is not given in "equal measure" beyond the minimum saving grace. This discriminate bestowal of grace beyond salvation to some more than others is the prerogative of a sovereign, or "supreme," God:

> That an equal portion of grace should not be extended to all, is attributable to the supreme will of God; that there are none to whom he does not vouchsafe grace sufficient for their salvation is attributable to his justice.
>
> CE, XIV, pp. 147 and 149

Sovereignly, with no respect of man's opinions, God bestows gifts on some men for special service by the same grace with which He saves them. In this view, there is no distinction between spiritual and non-spiritual concerns in life; everything is spiritual because everything is affected by the activity of God's grace in men's lives. Poetic composition, therefore, is as spiritual an activity for Milton as any other activity -- such as preaching or administering a Latin Secretaryship, for instance. Poetry is a valid medium with which to express love to God.

Indeed, Milton thought of his ability to write poetry as the most important talent that he could use to express his devotion to God. In The Reason of Church Government Urged Against Prelaty, which he wrote in 1642, Milton clearly identifies God as the source of his poetic talents:

> These abilities [to write religious poetry], wheresoever they
> be found, are the inspired gift of God, rarely bestowed, but
> yet to some (though most abuse) in every nation.
>   Hughes, p. 669

The ability to write poetry is the "inspired gift of God." Milton maintains throughout his career that his poetic talent is the gift of God. In accepting that God is the source of his poetic talent, Milton shoulders the concomitant responsibility that his abilities bring: he must not "abuse" the gift by not serving God with it; rather, he must make of his poetry an act of devotion to God.

Milton's belief that God enables him to write poetry is made more poignant by his awareness that not every one so gifted uses the talent for God's glory. When Michael presents the first human arts to Adam in Book Eleven of Paradise Lost, for instance, he tells Adam that Lamech's children abused their artistic abilities. They did not use them for God's glory, but for their own gain. Michael says in part:

> studious they appear
> Of arts that polish Life, Inventors rare,

> Unmindful of their Maker, though his Spirit
> Taught them, but they his gifts acknowledg'd none.
>
> XI, ll. 609-12

Milton repeats his concern about the abuse of art in <u>Paradise Regained</u> when the Son rejects Satan's temptation of Gentile culture:

> Alas! what can they [Gentiles] teach, and not mislead;
> Ignorant of themselves, of God much more,
> And how the world began, and how man fell
> Degraded by himself, on grace depending?
> Much of the Soul they talk, but all awry,
> And in themselves seek virtue, and to themselves
> All glory arrogate, to God give none,
> Rather accuse him under usual names,
> Fortune and Fate, as one regardless quite
> Of mortal things. Who therefore seeks in these
> True wisdom, finds her not . . .
>
> IV, ll. 309-19a

The Son's condemnation of the Gentile arts in general is a serious one in Milton's view because they have failed to teach wisdom. "True wisdom" is to know God -- His creation of men and His grace in their lives. With so many poets, in Milton's thinking, not using their abilities to serve God, Milton is particularly careful that he serve God with his poetry.[6]

In order for him to be able to write well, Milton knows that he must develop his talent. In <u>The Reason of Church Government</u>, for instance, he notes that in addition to his moral purification "must be added industrious and select reading, steady observation, insight into all seemly and generous arts and affairs" (p. 671). Milton is aware that he must read widely and judiciously, observe life carefully, and weigh the materials wisely -- if he is to write well enough to glorify God. He must work hard to perfect the talent that God has given him.

But his talent and training are not sufficient for him to write the type of poetry that he wishes to write. He must be divinely-inspired as well as divinely-talented. As he states of inspiration in The Reason of Church Government, the poet must apply himself

> by devout prayer to that eternal Spirit who can enrich with all utterance and knowledge, and sends out his seraphim with the hallowed fire of his altar, to touch and purify the lips of whom he pleases.
>
> p. 671

Clearly, Milton emphasizes his need for prayer to ask God to help him to write poetry. He goes on immediately to reiterate, however, his own need for "industry" in order for him to write well. In Milton's view, both inspiration and industry are necessary for a poet to write effective religious poetry.

In John Milton: Poet, Priest and Prophet, John Spencer Hill notes a valuable distinction between poetic talent and divine inspiration in Paradise Lost. Hill identifies the "Muse" in Paradise Lost as "the divinely implanted poetic talent . . . which Milton has possessed from birth and which he has nurtured and improved over a long life of study and severe application" and the "Spirit" of the invocations in Paradise Lost as the one who "purif [ies] the vessel [the poet] and enlightens [him] with knowledge that is unattainable except by direct revelation" (p. 110). Hill sees a two-fold dynamic at work in Paradise Lost: Milton's own poetic talent on the one hand and the divine, supernatural inspiration of the poet on the other, both of which are necessary for Milton to write poetry to the glory of God. When the poet in Paradise Lost asks for inspiration, therefore, we must assume that such an invocation is more than a literary convention because he sees himself as sinful and unable to write effectively; he asks for an inspiration that he feels he actually needs. Hill notes that "for Milton, inspiration is neither the anti-rational afflatus of the Corybantic priests in Plato's Ion 534a nor (at the other extreme) is it merely an empty rhetorical trope" (p. 60).

Milton knew that he needed inspiration to write poetry that was acceptable to God as an act of his devotion and he asks for that inspiration in most of his poems from the "Nativity Ode" on.

The "Nativity Ode" is an early example of a poem in which the poet asks for divine inspiration to assist him to express his love for God. The poet is grateful for the incarnation of the savior at Bethlehem. He begins with a prelude that invokes a "heav'nly Muse" for inspiration to lift the poet up to write a hymn of praise to the new-born King. He speaks to his Muse in these two stanzas:

> Say Heav'nly Muse, shall not thy sacred vein
> Afford a present to the Infant God?
> Hast thou no verse, no hymn, or solemn strain,
> To welcome him to this his new abode,
> Now while the Heav'n by the Sun's team untrod
>   Hath took no print of the approaching light,
> And all the the spangled host keep watch in
>   squadrons bright?

> See how from far upon the Eastern road
> The Star-led Wizards haste with odors sweet:
> O run, prevent them with thy humble ode,
> And lay it lowly at his blessed feet;
> Have thou the honor first, thy Lord to greet,
>   And join thy voice unto the Angel Choir,
> From out his secret Altar toucht with
>   hallow'd fire.
>   ll. 15-28

The poet asks his Muse for inspiration to "prevent," or precede, the Magi with a gift of a hymn for "the Infant God." This is both a request for divine aid to write the hymn and, as Woodhouse notes in The Poet and His Faith, a dedication of the hymn itself to God.[7] By seeking divine inspiration and by dedicating himself to God, Milton clearly declares himself a Christian poet in this prelude. Hill comments on the obvious sincerity in Milton's self-dedication to God in the "Nativity Ode":

> In the "Nativity Ode" Milton thinks of himself as a stylus dei, an amanuensis of deity. And while it is true that this stance, like the pagan afflatus of the earlier pieces, is sanctioned by a long tradition, the sincere and confident tone of the "Nativity Ode" makes it plain that the inspiration to which it lays claim is far from being a conventional literary topos.
>
> p. 59

Though the ode makes use of conventional materials, Hill maintains that its prelude indicates that Milton sees himself in need of divine aid if he is to write poetry that expresses love for God.

Some fourteen years after he wrote the "Nativity Ode," Milton comments in The Reason of Church Government on his need for inspiration in his poetry. In this passage, Milton refers specifically to his promise of Paradise Lost:

> Neither do I think it shame to covenant with any knowing reader, that for some years yet I may go on trust with him toward the payment of what I am now indebted, as being a work not to be raised from the heat of youth, or the vapors of wine, like that which flows at waste from the pen of some vulgar amorist, or the trencher fury of a riming parasite, nor to be obtained by the invocation of Dame Memory and her Siren daughters, but by devout prayer to that eternal Spirit who can enrich with all utterance and knowledge, and sends out his seraphim with the hallowed fire of his altar, to touch and purify the lips of whom he pleases.
>
> p. 671

Milton rejects secular subjects such as "vulgar" love poems called up by "Dame Memory and her Siren Daughters" and embraces instead "that eternal Spirit" who can inspire his poetry heavenward. The "Spirit" to whom Milton alludes here is the Holy Spirit who "sends out his seraphim with the hallowed fire of his altar, to touch and purify the lips of whom he [the Spirit] pleases." Seraphim are traditionally associated with purification.[8] As Merritt Y. Hughes notes, this is clearly a reference to Isaiah 6: 1-9.[9] This inspiration is literal for Milton in that the Spirit provides him with "knowledge" -- presumably about God and His action in human life. Such knowledge is beyond natural human talent; it comes from God.

Besides providing inspiration, the Spirit purifies the poet with "fire" from the "altar." In the passage from Isaiah to which Milton alludes, Isaiah laments his sinfulness: "Then said I, Woe is me! for I am undone; because I am a man of unclean lips." Because of his sinfulness, Isaiah is cleansed by God: God lays the "live coal" of purification upon Isaiah's lips (verse seven). He is then sent out to serve God (verse nine). All of this detail from Isaiah provides a source for Milton's understanding of inspiration in The Reason of Church Government. He regards himself as sinful; therefore, he needs to be sanctified; and he needs to be sent out as a prophet of God's "message," as Isaiah was. Thus, he will be able to serve God. The inspiration which Milton invokes is emphatically divine. It lifts him to a level higher than is normally possible, to a height at which the poet, now like a prophet, can announce what God has done for him. It is this type of inspiration, along with his inborn poetic talents, that Milton needs to write poetry that is an act of devotion to God -- he needs supernatural enlightenment and purification.

The question of the identity of the Muse who inspires Milton is, of course, a much-debated one -- especially in Paradise Lost and Paradise Regained. It is not my intention to trace in this chapter the complex issue of the Muse's identity in those two poems; I shall consider some of the specific problems that the subject of the Muse's identity raises that are relevant to the subject of devotion in the discussion of each of the poems.

With the exception of Maurice Kelley, who suggests in <u>This Great Argument</u> that the Muse invoked in Book Three is merely the physical light which Milton had lost in his blindness,[10] critics generally agree that Milton sincerely sought something higher than himself to aid him in the writing of his poems to the glory of God. James Holly Hanford, for instance, argues in "That Shepherd who First Taught the Chosen Seed" that Milton was more interested in divine guidance itself than in the specific name of the one who provides that assistance.[11] More recently, in <u>The Christian Poet in "Paradise Lost"</u>, William G. Riggs holds that the Muse is neither the Holy Spirit nor the Son of God, but a spirit who "accompanies" them from the beginning of time and who inspires Milton at his point of writing. He writes, " . . . this 'overshadowing Spirit' is sent along with the Son and is, therefore, presumably not identical with him" (pp. 163-64). Perhaps Riggs has in mind the personified Wisdom of Proverbs 8: "The Lord possessed me in the beginning of his way, before his works of old," Wisdom says (verse twenty-two). She adds, "For whoso findeth me findeth life, and shall obtain favor of the Lord" (verse thirty-five). John Spencer Hill maintains in <u>John Milton: Poet, Priest and Prophet</u>:

> For Milton, inspiration is . . . the operation of a sanctifying grace that continuously nourishes and sustains those whom God has marked as His special servants. And, while Milton's sense of poetic calling deepens and sharpens considerably in the years separating the "Nativity Ode" from <u>Paradise Lost,</u> the image of the live coal laid by the seraph on Isaiah's lip remains the constant symbol (in a Coleridgean sense) of his poetic calling.
>
> pp. 60-61

Whatever identity they ascribe to his muse, critics agree that Milton finds a legitimate inspiration for his poetry outside of himself. It is this inspiration that assists him in writing of heavenly things.

The question of identity aside, what finally is Milton's view of inspiration in <u>Paradise Lost</u> and <u>Paradise Regained</u>? I find Hill's conclusion in <u>John Milton: Poet, Priest and Prophet</u> a particularly useful statement of how Milton's view of inspiration helps to make his poetry an act of devotion to God. Hill writes:

> Milton's experience as God's spokesman in the prose works taught him to place himself in the tradition of Old Testament prophecy. And in that tradition, . . . inspiration is distinct from irrational afflatus and, in fact, bears no relation to it. The prophets are men, free men, who voluntarily co-operate with God and consciously accept the service 'imposed' on them. They will to relax the will, in order to declare God's will. In the same way <u>Paradise Lost</u> is the record of the collaboration between Poet and God, that is, between a free speaker and the divine word. In the opening invocation these two figures are invoked separately: through the 'heavenly muse' Milton declares his own readiness to begin, and through the invocation to the Spirit he calls upon God to sustain and direct the work.
>
> In later invocations the two functions are fused, as is natural since there is no distinction between instrument and Word once the request for inspiration has been granted.
>
> pp. 111-12

Hill refers to Milton as God's "spokesman" in his prose works and His "prophet" in the poetry. I prefer to call Milton God's "prophet" in the prose works because he thinks of himself as preaching "God's Word" to his nation.[12] Hill's comment that Milton willingly cooperates with God also corroborates my perception of him as a prophet (for St. Paul said that "the spirits of the prophets are subject to the prophets," I Cor. 14:32).

In his poems, however, Milton does not preach the Word of God. Rather, he celebrates the glories of God and his love for Him. He does this through his talents and the divine inspiration that he has received. As Hill states, by the end of the Invocation to Book One of Paradise Lost, the poet has already received the inspiration he needs -- by faith -- from God. Therefore, because the poet has been inspired at the beginning of the poem, he can write his poetry as an acceptable act of devotion to God (again, by faith) -- after all, the poet believes that God has inspired its very composition. Hence, as a poet, Milton is more like a priest than a prophet: he celebrates his own devotion to God in his poetry, whereas he preaches it in his prose.

In his poems, Milton integrates devotion with narrative events and character development. As Arthur Sewell writes in A Study of Milton's Christian Doctrine:

> The poems report the more integral truth of Milton's spiritual development. They not only tell us what were the achievements of his spiritual inquiry, but they also embody the affections of his heart, his agonies, his inward struggles, during the very process of inquiry.
>
> p. 83

Milton's poems "embody" and develop the spiritual "affections of his heart." They are acts of devotion, or celebrations, for him within which his characters progressively develop their love for God in the narrative events of the poems. Milton's view of poetry, therefore, emphasizes character development because it is in the characters themselves that he presents devotion to God.

Milton's emphasis on devotion in his characters reflects the paradigm of Protestant meditation that Barbara Lewalski identifies in Protestant Poetics and the Seventeenth Century Religious Lyric. Lewalski notes that Protestant meditation lends itself to "psychological insight" and development:

. . . Protestant meditation did engage the mind in an effort to penetrate deeply into the motives and motions of the psyche, and also to understand the self as the very embodiment of the subject meditated upon. The Word was still made flesh, though now in the self of the meditator . . . . This emphasis contributed to the creation with a new depth and sophistication of psychological insight. . . .

p. 150

In Milton's devotion, as well as in Protestant meditation in general, the "self" is the "very embodiment of the subject meditated upon." That is, God (the "subject" and the "Word" of Lewalski's statement) ascribes His characteristics to the character in the poem (the "self" and the "flesh" of the reference). Through the experiences of the narrative events in the poem, the characters acquire a love for God by developing certain qualities in their lives. This is how the "Word" becomes "flesh" . . . in the self of the "meditator" in Milton's poetry. The development of character in the course of a poem, therefore, is toward devotional love for God. Milton's contribution to devotional poetry is this development of devotion within a narrative sequence of events. In Milton's hands, devotion is no longer restricted to brief lyrics; it is an integral part of the epic (Paradise Lost and Paradise Regained) and drama (Samson Agonistes).

As we indicated in the introduction, Milton defines devotional love for God "above all other objects of affection" (CE, XVII, pp. 51 and 53). To love God, in Milton's view, is consciously to choose Him -- by a free-will act of faith -- above everything else as deserving of love. In The Christian Doctrine, Milton identifies seven different ways to express devotion to God; he names them "devout affections." These seven devout affections are trust, hope, gratitude, fear, humility, patience and obedience (CE, XVII, p. 51). They are the results, or "effects" as he calls them, of an individual's devotional love for God; they are the particular, active expressions of that love to God.

In The Christian Doctrine, Milton defines each of these devout affections, beginning with trust. He characterizes trust in God "as an effect of love . . . whereby we wholly repose on him [God]" (CE, XVII, p. 53). He distinguishes trust from faith in that, whereas faith has to do with a person's justification," or salvation, trust has to do with a Christian's daily confidence in God's goodness toward him. Such a trust is active and pragmatic; Milton cites three practical details which we can trust to God. He quotes Psalm 18: 2 and 3, "Jehovah is my rock and fortress . . . in whom I will trust," in order to indicate that God will protect us. Second, God will guide us. Referring to Psalm 37:5, "Commit thy way unto Jehovah, trust also in him and he shall bring it to pass," Milton states his trust that God will direct our lives. Third, God will "establish" our thoughts (Milton refers to Proverbs 16:3 in this regard) so as to stabilize our lives (CE, XVII, pp. 53 and 55). Milton's understanding of trust, then, is three-fold: God protects us from physical harm; He guides the direction of our lives; and He stabilizes our reason.

With trust comes hope, "that by which we expect with certainty the fulfillment of God's promises" (CE, XVII, p. 57). This is the certainty that what God promised in the Bible, He will perform in a Christian's life. Milton quotes Job 13:15, "though he [God] slay me, yet will I trust in him," to underscore his hope in God's love. He goes on to distinguish three benefits which result from the expression of devout hope. We are assured of life after death. We will be joyful because "the hope of the righteous shall be gladness" (Proverbs 10:28). And we will be strengthened, as Isaiah 40:31 promises: "they that wait upon the Lord shall renew their strength . . . ." These are all references which Milton cites to demonstrate that an individual's hope in God is safely founded and amply repaid (CE, XVIII, pp. 57 and 59). Each person must, of his own free will, choose to hope in the promise of God; when he does so, God not only fulfills his promises to him, but He also rewards his hope with eternal life, gladness and strength.

Because God is faithful to fulfill the promises which hope expects to have fulfilled, we are to be grateful toward Him. Milton defines gratitude as "that whereby we acknowledge his [God's] goodness in conferring benefits upon creatures so unworthy as ourselves" (CE, XVII, p. 59). There are two important thoughts here. First, God's goodness prompts our gratitude. Second, our sinfulness, which renders us unworthy of God's benefits, accentuates God's goodness. The scriptural passages which Milton quotes regarding gratitude relate to God's goodness in salvation. For example, I Corinthians 6:20, "Ye are bought with a price; therefore, glorify God in your body, and in your spirit, which are God's" expresses the Protestant teaching that Christ "paid" all of man's "sin-debt" in His death. We can add nothing to Christ's work. How are we to respond to such a benefit? With gratitude, Milton asserts, "let us have grace whereby we may serve God with reverence and godly fear" (Hebrews 12:28). Here again, as he does with hope and trust, Milton presents gratitude as an active and practical devout affection -- active and practical service to reflect the deliberate free-will choice of God above all other objects of affection.

Even in his depiction of devout fear, Milton declares that a devotional love of God is the only basis on which we are to reverence God. He says, "We are to reverence God as the supreme Father and Judge of all men, and dread offending him above all things" (CE, XVII, p. 61). First of all, Milton speaks of God as the Father here, a positive picture of God as the giver and sustainer of life and all its benefits. He cites Proverbs 19:23, "the fear of Jehovah tendeth to life," as evidence. This statement relates primarily to God's provision of our physical needs, though it may allude to spiritual life as well. Milton's next mention of God as the Judge of all men cites I Peter 1:17 as evidence that God will judge every man "according to [his] work." Because God is both preserver and judge, we are to reverence, or fear, the one who has that power over us. He loves us, but will judge our works.

If we fear God, we "acknowledge our unworthiness in [His] sight" (CE, XVII, p. 65). This acknowledgement is humility. Because of God's mercies to us, not because of His wrath against our sinfulness, we are to humble ourselves before Him. Milton quotes Genesis 32:10, "I am not worthy of the least of all thy mercies," to underscore the idea that our humility is to be predicated on the mercies we receive. In his quotation of Paul in I Timothy 1:15, "Christ Jesus came into the world to save sinners, of whom I am chief," Milton makes it clear that the greatest mercy of all is salvation. God's offer of salvation is what prompts the devout humility of The Christian Doctrine.

Closely related to hope in Milton's thinking is patience as a type of devotional love to God. "Patience is that whereby we acquiesce in the promises of God," he writes, "through a confident reliance on his divine providence, power, and goodness, and bear inevitable evils with equanimity, as the dispensation of the supreme Father, and sent for our good" (CE, XVII, p. 67). Because of His omnipotence, God can allow "inevitable evils" in our lives; because of His goodness, however, He will uphold us when the evil times come. Therefore, we are to love God with a patient love, not accusing Him of unkindness in the difficult times. Milton quotes many passages to substantiate his definition of patience, the most significant of which is Hebrews 10:36: "Ye have need of patience, that after ye have done the will of God, ye might receive the promise." Patience is necessary to hope, else the waiting upon God for Him to fulfill His promises would be too burdensome. Rooted in his conviction that God is faithful, Milton's devout patience is practical fortitude for daily living.

Obedience is Milton's final devout affection. He defines it as "that virtue whereby we propose to ourselves the will of God as the paramount rule of our conduct, and serve him alone" (CE, XVII, p. 69). Obedience is the end of devout love; it is the deliberate act of subordinating the human will to God's will in active service, an expression of love to God. Milton indicates that we are to obey God by quoting Christ in John 14:15: "If ye love me keep my commandments"; and I John 5:17: "He that doeth the will of God abideth for ever." Obedience testifies to our discipleship and it secures eternal life.

These seven devout affections -- trust, hope, gratitude, fear, humility, patience, and obedience -- are all different expressions of the love that Milton holds we are to have toward God. This love deliberately chooses God above all other objects of affection; these devout affections manifest that love to God in our experience. Milton writes poetry to express his devotion for God. Through the events in his major poems, he depicts his characters and speakers in such a way as to develop this kind of devotional love in their experiences.

Before the successful integration of devotion and narrative development that he achieves in Paradise Lost, Paradise Regained and Samson Agonistes, however, Milton writes many poems and prose works that do not express mature devotion to God. Milton develops his perception of devotion early in his poetic career -- specifically between 1629 and 1637, I would suggest. The "Nativity Ode" (and its related poem, the "Elegy to Diodati") and "The Passion" are the first poems to express any of these specific devout affections. Of course, the subject of the "Nativity Ode" is religious -- as is the subject of "The Passion" -- and lends itself to a devotional tone. However, Milton develops his mature expression of devotion first in "Lycidas," a poem not specifically "religious" in subject-matter. The occasion of "Lycidas" is not an event in the life of a biblical character; the occasion of the poem is the inexplicable, premature death of a fellow-poet. As the poet confronts the death of Lycidas, Milton writes his first fully devotional poem. These three poems, and Milton's development of devotion in them, are the subject of the next chapter.

Notes
Chapter One

[1]John Milton, "At a Solemn Music," <u>John Milton: Complete Poems and Major Prose</u>, Edited by Merritt Y. Hughes (New York: The Odyssey Press, 1957), pp. 81-82. All subsequent references to Milton's poetry and prose (with the exception of <u>The Christian Doctrine</u>) are to this edition.

[2]John Hollander, <u>The Untuning of the Sky: Ideas of Music in English Poetry, 1500-1700</u> (Princeton: Princeton University Press, 1969), p. 324.

[3]Compare Milton's comment in <u>The Reason of Church Government</u>, Hughes p. 670: "Teaching over the whole book of sanctity and virtue through all the instances of example, with such delight to those especially of soft and delicious temper who will not so much as look upon Truth herself, unless they see her elegantly dressed . . . ."

[4]cf. Sewell, p. 19: "true regeneration itself is 'supernatural' and the 'inward man' is created 'afresh,' the 'old man being destroyed'."

[5]cf. CE, XIV, p. 91: "It has been the practice of the schools to use the word predestination, not only in the sense of election, but also of reprobation. This is not consistent with the caution necessary on so momentous a subject, since wherever it is mentioned in Scripture, election alone is uniformly intended."

[6]Milton writes in <u>The Reason of Church Government</u> that he wishes his poetry "to be an interpreter and relater of the best and sagest things among [his] own citizens . . . .

[7]A.S.P. Woodhouse, <u>The Poet and His Faith: Religion and Poetry in England from Spenser to Eliot and Dryden</u> (Chicago: University of Chicago Press, 1965), p. 92. All subsequent references to this work will be cited in the text of the book.

[8]Riggs, p. 86.

[9]Hughes, p. 671, note 179.

[10]Maurice Kelley, This Great Argument: A Study of Milton's "De Doctrina Christiana" as a Gloss upon "Paradise Lost" (Princeton: Princeton University Press, 1941), p. 92.

[11]James Holly Hanford, "That Shepherd who First Taught the Chosen Seed," University of Toronto Quarterly, VII (1939), pp. 403-19.

[12]cf. note 6: for Milton, poetry is "an interpreter and relater of the best and sagest things. . . ."

CHAPTER TWO
Early Poems

As early as 1628 and 1629, Milton begins to indicate that he wishes to write specifically "Christian" poetry. It is in his poetry that he first confronts the problems that writing Christian poetry presents. For Milton, the major problem is the question of the relationship between religious subjects -- such as the events of Christ's life, for example -- and classical literature. In "At a Vacation Exercise," which he wrote in 1628, Milton communicates some dissatisfaction with his "muse" for alluding exclusively to classical materials (the particular references in the poem are to Apollo, Hebe, Neptune and Ulysses -- all "deities" whom the speaker of the poem sees in "heaven"). "But fie, my wand'ring Muse," the speaker scolds, "how thou dost stray! Expectance calls thee another way" (ll. 53-54). Even at this point in the poem, however, the speaker cites yet another classical reference, namely the Aristotelian "predicaments." Nevertheless, Milton is conscious of a tension in his poetry between classical materials and "some graver subject" (l. 30). He eventually resolves this tension by writing about Christian not classical heroes, beginning with the "Infant God" in the "Nativity Ode." John Spencer Hill characterizes "At a Solemn Music" as a public "manifesto" of Milton's religious intentions for his English poetry.[1] In December of 1629, a year and a half after the "Vacation Exercise," Milton announces in "Elegy VI" his specific plans to write devotional poetry.

In "Elegy VI" (to Diodati), Milton writes a clear declaration of his intent to write devotional poetry that will express his love for God in a variety of ways. Milton's first concern in this elegy is that the devotional poet be morally pure, "innocent of crime and chaste, his conduct irreproachable and his hands stainless" (ll. 68-71). These lines impose strict moral standards on the poet who wishes to write on divine themes; Milton's devotional poet must be entirely blameless. As we noted in the first chapter, Milton's ideal poet is poetically talented, divinely inspired, and well practised in his writing. Here in "Elegy VI," Milton adds to those demands the requirement of moral purity. When at the conclusion of the Elegy, Milton announces his intention to write the "Nativity Ode," he leaves the reader with the impression that he is the morally-pure poet who will write devotional poetry.

The announcement at the end of "Elegy VI" that Milton is writing a poem as a "gift" for the Christ-child is the most important statement in Milton's early poetry that he has chosen to write devotional poetry. The final two verse paragraphs of the Elergy are clearly a dedication of his poetry to God:

> But if you will know what I am doing (if only you think it of any importance to know whether I am doing anything) -- I am singing the heaven-descended King, the bringer of peace, and the blessed times promised in the sacred books -- the infant cries of our God and his stabling under a mean roof who, with his Father, governs the realms above. I am singing the starry sky and the hosts that sang high in air, and the gods that were suddenly destroyed in their own shrines.
> These are my gifts for the birthday of Christ -- gifts which the first light of its dawn brought to me. For you these simple strains that have been meditated on my native pipes are waiting; and you, when I recite them to you, shall be my judge.
>
> ll. 78-90

As the reference to the fact that the "Nativity Ode" was written in the "first light" of Christmas morning that year indicates, "Elegy VI" was written shortly after Christmas in 1629. Clearly, Milton regards the "Nativity Ode" to be a song in praise of the incarnation of Christ.

In offering the "Nativity Ode" as a "song" of praise to the newborn king, Milton associates himself with the Hebrew priest of old who celebrated his "sacrifices of praise" (Hebrew 13:15) to God. In her book, Images and Themes in Five Poems by Milton, Rosemond Tuve refers to the "Nativity Ode" as a "liturgical act of praise."[2] While I do not wish to assert that the "Nativity Ode" is liturgical, I do wish to emphasize Milton's perception of himself as a "priest" and his poem as a "gift" to God. In "Elegy VI," Milton speaks of the "bard," or poet, as the "priest" of the gods (l. 77); the poet is an intermediary between men and the gods. In the "Nativity Ode," Milton regards himself as one who celebrates the birth of Christ.

The "Nativity Ode" specifically celebrates the incarnation of Christ, "the heaven-descended King" of Bethlehem's manger. The poet begins the hymn proper with a picture of the nativity scene:

> It was the Winter wild,
> While the Heav'n-born child,
> > All meanly wrapt in the rude manger lies;
> Nature in awe to him
> Had doff't her gaudy trim,
> > With her great Master so to sympathize.
> > > ll. 29-34

The scene of the Christ-child "all meanly wrapt" emphasizes the "heav'n-born child['s]" humility in assuming a position of poverty as to be born in a "rude manger." The poet introduces the actual picture of the nativity scene with a reference to "the Star-led Wizards," or Magi of the second chapter of Matthew's Gospel account, and concludes it with Mary's maternal solicitations for the sleepy child by "[laying] her Babe to rest." It is a traditional picture, though not given in much detail.

There is, however, a second subject in the "Nativity Ode," one which accounts more for the devotional tone in the poem than do the events of the incarnation and nativity. This is the subject of redemption. Christ was born to die to "redeem" men. The prelude to the "Nativity Ode" begins with the poet's consciousness of the dual focus of Christ's birth and redemptive death:

> This is the Month, and this the happy morn
> Wherein the Son of Heav'n's eternal King,
> Of wedded Maid and Virgin Mother born,
> Our great redemption from above did bring.
>
> ll. 1-4

The poet projects a picture of Calvary on Bethlehem, anticipating Christ's crucifixion and the salvation, or "redemption," that it would bring.

The poet refers again to the crucifixion in stanza sixteen of the hymn itself. In the fifteenth stanza, the poet presents an eschatological view of the final victory of "Truth," "Justice" and "Mercy." As he begins the sixteenth stanza, however, he acknowledges that "This [victory] must not yet be so" because Christ has not yet finished the work that will make that future victory possible. It is clear in the stanza that Christ must suffer at Calvary before He can reign as King:

> The Babe lies yet in smiling Infancy,
> That on the bitter cross
> Must redeem our loss;
> So both himself and us to glorify.
>
> ll. 152-55

Though the baby is "smiling" now, he will suffer on the "bitter" cross of Calvary in just a few years. The telos of the incarnation is the crucifixion. The "Babe [who] lies yet in smiling Infancy" in the "Nativity Ode" must go to the "bitter cross / To redeem our loss." As a result of His death at Calvary,

Christ finally binds "Th'old Dragon under ground," thereby glorifying himself and all who are redeemed. But this victory is begun, the poet emphasizes, on "this happy day" of the nativity. There is, therefore, a dual focus to the "Nativity Ode," a focus on both incarnation and crucifixion. The poem is as much a prophecy of the cross as it is a celebration of the manger.

The double focus on Christ's birth and death in the Ode accounts for the experience of devotion in the poem. The poet expresses his love for God in the "Nativity Ode" as hope -- hope that, because God has been faithful in providing the promised incarnation, so too will He be faithful in providing redemption, or salvation. Both poles of Christ's life are necessary for the poet's hope to be valid; the hope of redemption is predicated on the fact of the nativity. Christ's incarnation is both the fulfillment of many Old Testament prophecies[3] and also a promise of the climactic event of the New Testament, the crucifixion. Therefore, because it faithfully fulfills Old Testament prophecies, the nativity gives testimony to the certainty of redemption at Calvary. It is the assurance that God will perform what He promises that is the major characteristic of Milton's devout affection of hope in The Christian Doctrine: "hope," he writes, "is that [affection] by which we expect with certainty the fulfillment of God's promises" (CE, XVII, p. 57). It is this confident expectation that is the speaker's experience of devotion in the poem.

There is another side to the hope which the poet experiences in the "Nativity Ode," and that is the dismissal of doubt. Doubt is one of two opposites to hope as Milton defines it in The Christian Doctrine, the other being despair (CE, XVII, p. 59). The extremity of despair does not enter the "Nativity Ode," but victory over doubt is certainly a part of the devotional experience in the poem. Behind the necessity for the incarnation is Satan's victory in the garden of Eden in effecting the fall into sin of Adam and Eve. As a result of this victory, Satan enjoys a certain "sway" over the earth and its inhabitants -- until the incarnation, that is.

Stanza eighteen makes it clear how significant the nativity is in dispelling the poet's concern that Satan's "usurped" power is eternal:

> And then at last our bliss
> Full and perfect is,
>> But now begins, for from this happy day
> Th'old Dragon under ground,
> In straiter limits bound,
>> Not half so far casts his usurped sway,
> And wroth to see his Kingdom fail,
> Swinges the scaly Horror of his folded tail.
>> ll. 165-72

The birth of Christ "begins" the final defeat of Satan which will be completed at Calvary.

Surely the many years between the fall in Eden and the nativity in Bethlehem discouraged hope that God would ever "bruise [the serpent's] head" as He promised he would (Genesis 3:15); would God ever vindicate His Word? By placing himself in the company of eyewitnesses to the birth of Christ, the poet in the Ode experiences the release from doubt in God which the nativity brings:

> This is the Month, and this the happy morn
> Wherein the Son of Heav'n's eternal King,
> Of wedded Maid, and Virgin Mother born,
> Our great redemption from above did bring;
> For so the holy sages once did sing,
>> That he our deadly forfeit should release,
> And with his Father work us a perpetual peace.
>> ll. 1-7

This is "the happy morn" that all the "holy sages" of old celebrated in anticipation only. The poet of the Ode is the first to celebrate the actual end to the doubt that God would never fulfill His promise of the incarnation and the beginning of the realization of the hope for redemption that Messiah's birth brings -- he "prevents," or precedes, the "Star-led Wizards" to the manager. (The poet even reports the shepherds' experience of the music of the spheres "on the Lawn / Or ere the point of dawn" as if he had observed it.) The poet experiences devotion in the poem in the form of the hope that the nativity inaugurates.

The poet stands as eyewitness to a major event in God's dealings with man -- an event second only to the crucifixion in the divine redemptive purposes. How is he to be worthy to celebrate the nativity in his poetry? The subject of redemption is so holy that the poet's final request in the prelude to the Hymn is for his sin to be cleansed: he wishes "from out his secret Altar [to be] toucht with hallowed fire." Like Isaiah of old, the poet's lips must be purged of sin by the seraph if he is to write of such a high subject. Isaiah states, "Woe is me! . . . because I am a man of unclean lips." Understanding his sinfulness, he asks for cleansing: "Then flew one of the seraphim unto me, having a live coal in his hand . . . And he laid it upon my mouth, and said, 'Lo, this hath touched thy lips; and thine iniquity is taken away' " (Isaiah 6:5-7). The allusion in the prelude to the "hallow'd fire," therefore, emphasizes the poet's consciousness that God must make him pure so that he is a fit priest to celebrate the hymn of praise to "the Infant God."

Personal purity, however important to the poet in the "Nativity Ode" and to Milton throughout his life, is inadequate by itself to assure the poet's "fitness" for the hymn. He must also be inspired by God. This is especially so in that, by making the poet an eyewitness of the nativity which begins the New Testament, Milton denies the poet access to the New Testament writings which teach the redemptive purpose of Christ's birth; at the point of the poet's writing his song of praise, the New Testament had not yet been written. The poet must receive the revelation of Christ's death supernaturally, therefore, by inspiration from God -- just as the apostles themselves did.

In addition, the poet's sinful nature makes his need for divine inspiration even more poignant. Were he not sinful, he would have no need of redemption and, therefore, no need to compose a hymn of praise for the incarnation. Had Adam and Eve not sinned (and, in them, all men), no savior would have been necessary; hence, neither Bethlehem nor Calvary would have been necessary either. The subject of redemption presumes a fallen poet who needs to be raised up to the subject's height. Therefore, the poet seeks divine inspiration to lift him up to be equal to the task. He writes in his introductory invocation:

> Say Heav'nly Muse, shall not thy sacred vein
> Afford a present to the Infant God?
> Hast thou no verse, no hymn, or solemn strain,
> To welcome him to this his new abode?
>
> ll. 15-18

The poet asks for inspiration from a "heavenly muse," presumably the Holy Spirit, simply because he is a fallen man who has lost the intimate communion with God that Adam and Eve had before the fall. Hence, the speaker in the poem introduces his hymn with a twofold request of God: first, to cleanse him from sin; and, second, to inspire his hymn of praise so that it will be an acceptable gift to lay at Christ's "blessed feet." By superimposing Calvary on Bethlehem, Milton creates a more adequate experience of devotion than a simple religious poem on the nativity alone would give.

The importance of the "Nativity Ode" in developing the experience of devotion is twofold. First, Milton makes it clear in this ode that a poem is not devotional simply because it has a religious subject (such as the birth of Christ). As we have shown, devotion in the "Nativity Ode" does not come from the divine birth alone. Second, devotion is an experience of a person within the poem itself. In the "Nativity Ode," the poet expresses a devout hope for redemption on the basis of the incarnation. The "Nativity

Ode" establishes that, for Milton, devotion is a dynamic hope of the poet in the poem; in the later narrative poems, the characters -- Adam and Eve in Paradise Lost, the Son in Paradise Regained, and Samson in Samson Agonistes -- are the ones who experience devotion.

Three months after he wrote the "Nativity Ode," Milton returned to a religious subject, this time Christ's passion and crucifixion in "The Passion." As Hanford indicates, it is clear that Milton intended "The Passion" to be a sequel to the "Nativity Ode," though the date of March 1630 (not Hanford's April 1630) is the correct date, March having been the month of Easter that year:[4]

> "The Passion" immediately follows "On the Morning of Christ's Nativity" in the 1645 edition and apparently belongs to the following Easter (i.e., April, 1630). It is bound to the preceding work by allusions in the opening lines and by the use of a meter identical with that employed in the introductory portion of the other. The poem represents an attempt to continue the lofty religious vein which Milton had entered upon in earnest of his new consecration in 1629. Quite possibly he projected such a series of commemorations of the divine events at their appropriate anniversaries in the Church calendar as are to be found among the works of Herbert and Donne.
>
> pp. 144-45

No doubt Milton thought of "Upon the Circumcision," written two years later, as a part of the same "series of commemorations of the divine events" of Christ's earthly life. However, he was unable to finish "The Passion." At the end of the fragment, Milton writes, "This subject the Author finding to be above the years he had, when he wrote it, and nothing satisfied with what was begun, left it unfinisht" (p. 63). He felt too immature to write well about such a profound subject.

Why did "The Passion" not satisfy Milton? What internal weaknesses are there that would indicate why the poem failed? I think that there are three areas of weakness in "The Passion" which account for Milton's inability to write effectively, all of which ultimately suggest that the poet lacked a sufficient devotional perspective in the poem. While Milton's subject is certainly the most "religious" of all possible subjects, he does not approach it with a consistently devotional attitude. Hence, the poem collapses.

The first problem is that the poet relies too much on classical literature in the poem. In stanza two, for instance, the poet speaks of Christ as the conventional classical hero:

> Most perfect Hero, tried in heaviest plight
> Of labors huge and hard, too hard for human sight.
>
> ll. 12-13

Christ is a Herculean figure who shows his deity by his "labors huge and hard." The heroic conventions in classical and Renaissance literature demanded that a poet "overgo" all other men in the figure of his hero. Milton is writing within this tradition in "The Passion," just as he is in the "Nativity Ode" in the reference to Christ's defeating "th'old Dragon" and all of his imps. The difference between the Hercules myth in the "Nativity Ode" and its use in "The Passion" is that Milton does not progress beyond the myth, or, more importantly, synthesize the myth with the Christian tradition in the "The Passion" as he does in the "Nativity Ode." Although Christ is an anti-type of Hercules, His excellencies are a matter of the superlative degree in "The Passion." The sacrifice at Calvary, however, is traditionally regarded as a matter of Christ's divine nature, not of human courage. Orthodox Christianity claims that the divine God-man died on the cross and rose again. Milton's depiction of Christ as a super-hero falls short of the biblical claim that Christ is divine. Therefore, the death on the cross would become merely another heroic action of a good man, not a substitutionary atonement. The youthful Milton could not present the Son of God in the classical mode as being more human than divine; and this is one reason he felt unequal to the task.

The second problem of "The Passion" is its reliance in the penultimate stanza on icons instead of a consistent focus on the person of Christ himself. In this stanza, the speaker "sees" the tomb of Christ and elevates it almost to the status of veneration. It is "that sad sepulchral rock / That was the Casket of Heav'n's richest store" that provides the subject for the stanza. The poet wishes to write his "[com]plaining verse" actually on the tomb -- making it almost like the Hebrew wailing wall in Jerusalem where Jews go to have their prayers answered. He makes of the tomb a shrine to be esteemed as holy. This stanza is the closest that the poet comes in the fragment to iconography; he focuses more on the object of the tomb than on the person of Christ. Therefore, a devotional attitude is entirely out of place -- at least for a Protestant poet it is. The proper subject of devotion for Milton is God. Hence he cannot continue the poem with its emphasis on the tomb rather than on Christ.

Not only do classical mythology and Christian icons not grant an adequate vehicle for Calvary, neither does Christian mysticism. Stanza six is a mystical vision like Ezekiel's:

> See, see the Chariot and those rushing wheels
> That whirl'd the Prophet up at Chebar flood;
> My spirit some transporting Cherub feels,
> To bear me where the Towers of Salem [Jerusalem]
> stood,
> Once glorious Towers, now sunk in guiltless blood;
> There doth my soul in holy vision sit,
> In pensive trance, and anguish, and ecstatic fit.
> ll. 36-42

The poet alludes to Ezekiel 1:16 in his reference to "Chebar flood," the river by which Ezekiel was given his vision of the great and small wheels. Like

Ezekiel, the poet "feels" himself enter into an "ecstatic fit" and "holy vision" which transports him to Jerusalem. There, he meditates in "pensive trance, and anguish" on the events about to be unfolded outside the city walls. Salem means peace. How is it, then, that the poet sees destruction and "guiltless blood" in his vision of Salem? He writes as if the events of the passion are still future. This is why it is necessary for the poet to be given a mystical vision, like the prophets of old, in order to see Calvary and the crucifixion; it is as if the crucifixion is still a future event. Herein lies the third problem of the poem: the eschatological vision of the cross without the resurrection is inconsistent with any valid sense of Christian devotion.

The underlying problem in "The Passion" is its emphasis on sorrow as opposed to hope. Sorrow is not consistent with a devotional experience that takes the Christian God into account. Sorrow can only be temporary because the climax of Christ's suffering is not the tomb, but the empty tomb. Hanford notes that Milton is, by temperament, "remot[e] from the emotion of religious sorrow" (p. 155); certainly the failure of "The Passion" is largely attributable to the poet's inability to project the hope of the resurrection through the sorrow of the cross. The "Nativity Ode" projects the hope of redemption through the certainty of the incarnation and thereby provides a successful devotional experience for the poet-speaker. "The Passion," however, fails because in it death is final; there is no hope for victory over death. Just as it is true that the religious subject of the birth of Christ does not make the "Nativity Ode" devotional, it is also true that the religious subject of the crucifixion alone does not give Milton an adequate basis for devotion. Because the poet's experience stops short of the resurrection, he is overcome with the horror of the cross and cannot continue the poem. "The Passion" remains "unfinisht" because its devotional experience is incomplete. There is no hope.

Milton resumes the narrative of Christ's death and carries it through to its conclusion in the resurrection, ascension and second advent in Paradise Lost, Book Twelve, lines 402 to 465. In Oaten Reeds and Trumpets: Pastoral and Epic in Virgil, Spenser and Milton (1981), Donald

M. Rosenberg suggests that this passage can be regarded as Milton's completion of the "The Passion" fragment.[5] The connection between the two pieces is a valuable one in that the speech in <u>Paradise Lost</u>, in contrast to "The Passion," moves toward gratitude for what God does through Christ. Michael is the speaker of the account which he addresses to Adam. He concludes his narrative to Adam that the earth will be a "far happier place" when Christ returns than Eden was before the fall. Adam responds to Michael with his hope in the certainty that God would defeat Satan and vindicate Himself strengthened:

> O goodness infinite, goodness immense!
> That all this good of evil shall produce,
> And evil turn to good; more wonderful
> Than that which by creation first brought forth
> Light out of darkness! full of doubt I stand,
> Whether I should repent me now of sin
> By mee done and occasion'd, or rejoice
> Much more, that much more good will to Men
> From God, and over wrath grace shall abound.
>
> XII, ll. 469-78

As he does throughout the whole of Michael's account, Adam stands here in a special position. By means of God's revealing history to him through Michael, Adam is able to know what he could not otherwise have known. All of Michael's narrative is eschatology to Adam; Michael's revelation of the course of human history confirms Adam's hope that God will reverse his failure. He rejoices "that all this good of evil shall produce, / And evil turn to good." Adam descants on the victory at Calvary; he does not lament suffering and death on the cross. He cannot bemoan Christ's suffering because Michael does not describe it in any detail; he merely announces that Christ will be

> to death condemn'd
> A shameful and accurst death, nail'd to the Cross

By his own Nation, slain for to bring Life.

XII, ll. 412b-14

Milton clearly avoids the sorrow of "The Passion" in <u>Paradise Lost</u>. Rather, he emphasizes the <u>telos</u> of that sorrow -- resurrection and redemption.[6] This section in <u>Paradise Lost</u>, therefore, provides the hope that "The Passion" did not provide.

Two other poems written between the "Nativity Ode" and "Lycidas" deserve attention for their expression of devotion. One is a religious poem, "Upon the Circumcision" (1632-33); the other is a non-religious poem, "Comus: a Mask" (1634). "Upon the Circumcision" is the third in a sequence of poems on the events of the life of Christ.[7] The poet attempts to make much of Jesus' circumcision in the poem, proclaiming it as a type of the crucifixion (the antitype). As He does on the cross, Christ here "bleeds to give us ease" because our "sin / Sore doth begin / His infancy to seize!" (ll. 11-14). In the Old Testament, the shedding of blood always accomplishes the remission of sins.[8] The blood that the circumcision sheds is necessitated by our sin. Christ's wound at the circumcision is the type of His crucifixion agony in the poem and it foreshadows the reference to the suffering at the conclusion of the poem:

but Oh! ere long
Huge pangs and strong
Will pierce more near his heart.

ll. 26-28

As in the "Nativity Ode," we have here the projection of the crucifixion of Christ through another, earlier event of the Savior's life. There is, therefore, a devotional experience in the life of the poet-speaker in "Upon the Circumcision"; there is hope that, just as the child suffers the pain of the circumcision, so too will he accept the agony of the crucifixion to redeem men.

Christ's obedience (also a subject of <u>Paradise Regained</u>) is the second devout affection of "Upon the Circumcision." The poet states that Christ "seals [His] obedience first with [the] wounding smart" of the circumcision itself. The occasion of the poem becomes a symbol of the Son's obedience to the Father. Because of Christ's obedient submission to the wound of circumcision, the poet experiences the certainty that He will be obedient at Calvary. Hence, the poet's hopes for his own redemption are strengthened by the assurance of Christ's foreshadowed death. "Upon the Circumcision" is the last of Milton's poems that celebrate the events of Christ's earthly life until he writes of the temptations in <u>Paradise Regained</u>.

The second poem that has devotional tones is "Comus: a Mask." "A Mask" of course is not a biblical poem in the same way that the "Nativity Ode", "The Passion" and "Upon the Circumcision" are; it does not present an event in Christ's life. However, as A.S.P. Woodhouse argues in <u>The Poet and His Faith</u>, it is a "spiritual" poem in that its subject is (at least in part) the conflict of nature and grace (p. 98). In regards to its devotional elements, "A Mask" is a transitional poem for Milton between the religious poetry on the events of Christ's life on the one hand and an integration, or synthesis, of devotion with other poetic elements on the other hand. Milton accomplishes the integration of devotion into his poetry first in "Lycidas." Of course, "A Mask" is much more than a "transitional" poem; it is an important poem in its own right. Rosemond Tuve claims that it "comes close to the perfection of 'Lycidas.' "[9]

If we accept Tillyard's position that the subject of the poem is chastity -- the Lady's chastity -- and, if we accept Woodhouse's association (p. 98) of the two brothers with nature and Sabrina with Grace,[10] then the final speech in the wood is more a retreat than a celebration. I have in mind these lines, the Spirit speaking to the Lady:

Come Lady, while Heaven lends us grace,
Let us fly this cursed place,

Lest the sorcerer us entice
With some other new device.

ll. 138-41

The agents of good in the poem have combined to rescue the Lady from Comus' seduction or, worse yet, his violation of her. The Brothers and the Spirit rescue her from physical harm; Sabrina releases her from the "spiritual," or mental, bondage of the curse. However, the Spirit still wishes to spare the Lady further temptation, counselling flight from the "cursed place." Surely the Spirit's suggestion of flight is a superficial response to the presence of evil in the universe. His advice implies that evil is limited in location and that a change in locale will eliminate its presence. This separation of good from evil in "A Mask" undermines any serious devotional elements that the poem may have; indeed, the failure of the poem to face evil as an omnipresent fact of this life renders devotion impossible.

However, the poem is after all a masque, a conventional set-piece that does not demand, or even allow, serious moral questioning. Milton deals with the subject of chastity in the poem either superficially within the masque tradition or allegorically. Rosemond Tuve's "Image, Form and Theme in 'A Mask,' " for example, argues that the poem is a moral allegory built "upon the great hinge of the Circe-Comus myth" (p. 116). But such an interpretation does not take into account the presence of real evil in the universe.

The problem of devotion in "A Mask" is that of Milton's Platonic separation of physical from ideal, of body from soul, as Mary Ann Radzinowicz states it in Toward "Samson Agonistes": the Growth of Milton's Mind.[11] She cites Milton's early distinction between body and soul as evidenced in "A Mask" in these lines:

things that no gross ear can hear,
Till oft converse with heav'nly habitants

Begin to cast a beam on th'outward shape,
The unpolluted temple of the mind,
And turns it by degrees to the soul's essence,
Till all be made immortal.

ll. 458-63

The body is "gross," the soul an immortal "essence." How can such a bifurcated being love a God who has no real presence in a world of evil? Later in his life, however, Milton changes his dualistic position and, in <u>The Christian Doctrine</u>, he teaches that body and soul are one:

> it is said . . . that "man became a living soul;" whence it may be inferred . . . that man is a living being, intrinsically and properly one and individual, not compound or separable, not, according to the common opinion, made up and framed of two distinct and different natures, as of soul and body, but that the whole man is soul, and soul man, that is to say, a body, or substance individual, animated, sensitive, and rational; and that the breath of life was neither a part of the divine essence, nor the soul itself, but as it were an inspiration of some divine virtue fitted for the exercise of life and reason, and infused into the organic body; for man himself, the whole man, when finally created, is called in express terms, "a living soul."

CE, XV, pp. 39 and 41

What Milton came to realize is that devotion to God is inadequate if it cannot face evil in this life. And, because of evil, death: "for the wages of sin is death," St. Paul writes (Romans 6:23). It is in his facing death in "Lycidas" three years after "A Mask" was written that Milton develops a devotional experience as an integral element within a poem.

In "Lycidas," Milton responds to the death by drowning of a friend and fellow-poet. As the poet-speaker in the poem expresses his grief over the loss of Lycidas, he begins to doubt God's benevolence. As he moves from one thought to another, however, the poet-speaker comes to experience a certain hope that, because God has given Lycidas immortality, so too will He grant the speaker immortality. As Mary Ann Radzinowicz states, there is a "conversion of [the speaker's] anxiety into assurance" (p. 142). The immortality of which the poem speaks is not a delusive "Fame" for the poet, for Lycidas died before he wrote his great poetry; it is rather the personal immortality of life after death "through the dear might of him that walk'd the waves" (l. 173). The process by which the poet-speaker realizes this hope in his own "life" accounts for the experience of devotion in the poem.

The pastoral elegy form which Milton chooses for "Lycidas" provides a "decent drapery of grief," as Hanford says (p. 167), and a degree of formality and objectivity. The poem is, in part, a public lament for Lycidas, a fellow "swain," having been printed as the final poem in the Iusta Eduardo King, the memorial volume for King. Many of the poem's details come from the elegaic tradition.[12] The pastoral elegy has a long and complex history with its conventions originating in Theocritus, Moschus, Bion and Virgil in classical antiquity and developed in Renaissance England by Edmund Spenser and many others. In addition to these classical and Renaissance sources, there are the biblical pastorals in Psalm Twenty-three and the tenth chapter of John's Gospel. The Johannine material is particularly relevant to the attack on the clergy in "Lycidas." Milton employs these precedents to provide a richness and diversity that allows the poet-speaker in the poem to modulate his grief and despair into hope. The hope which concludes "Lycidas," however, is not merely a superficial elegaic convention; it is also a personal expression of devotion on the speaker's part that is the climax of the devotional elements in the poem.

Because so much of "Lycidas" is conventional, some scholars have regretted the poem's "impersonal" nature. This is a serious charge if the poem is to be considered devotional, for it cannot express a valid love for

God if the problem of evil is avoided by merely de-personalizing the loss of a friend. Dr. Johnson leads the charge:

> One of the poems on which much praise has been bestowed is "Lycidas," of which the diction is harsh, the rhymes uncertain, and the numbers unpleasing. What beauty there is we must therefore seek in the sentiments and images. It is not to be considered as the effusion of real passion; for passion runs not after remote allusions and obscure opinions. Passion plucks no berries from the myrtle and ivy, nor calls upon Arethuse and Mincius, nor tells of rough satyrs and "fauns with cloven heel." Where there is leisure for fiction there is little grief. [13]

For Johnson, there is no "real passion" in "Lycidas"; its "remote allusions and obscure opinions" do not allow it. In our own century, as well, John Crowe Ransom insists that the poem is an impersonal "literary exercise." [14] Does the elegy, then, fall short of expressing real devotion because its conventions do not allow the poet-speaker to address the issue of death personally?

Not all scholars find the poem too impersonal, however. Some critics find the poem intensely personal. Richard P. Adams, for example, even in discussing "The Archetypal Pattern of Death and Rebirth in 'Lycidas,' " states:

> Milton was expressing his own feelings in "Lycidas," and not any abstract or general or public sorrow. The personal note established in the first five lines is maintained throughout. [15]

pp. 123-24

Adams flies directly in the face of Dr. Johnson by referring specifically to the myrtle and ivy (which Johnson found to betray insincerity) as examples of the poet's personal grief. E.M.W. Tillyard shifts the <u>locus</u> of the grief ingeniously by citing Milton, not Edward King, as the proper subject of the poem:

> Fundamentally "Lycidas" concerns Milton himself; King is but
> the excuse for one of Milton's more personal poems.[16]

If the poem is personal because it is "really" autobiographical, then do we have a basis on which to build a case for devotion in the poem? I think not. Milton's simply being the man behind the poem does not allow the devotion of the poem to exist within the poem because the experience of devotion would demand constant reference to the man Milton personally -- if Tillyard is correct, that is. I think that David Daiches is closer to an understanding of the experience of devotion in "Lycidas" when he argues that the "poet-priest" is the proper subject of the poem (p. 104).

It is the poet-speaker who comes to have the devotional experience of hope in "Lycidas." Milton makes use of the pastoral elements in order to express devotion throughout the poem, involving the speaker in both classical and biblical associations. As poet, the speaker is in the classical tradition; as priest, he is in the biblical tradition. David Daiches summarizes this confluence of the two traditions of the pastoral:

> The shepherd as the symbol of the spiritual leader [pastor-
> priest] is of course an old Christian usage, and goes right
> back to the Bible. But in the classical tradition the shepherd
> [poet] also sings and pipes. So by combining the Christian
> and classical traditions [in "Lycidas"] Milton can use the
> shepherd as a symbol for the combination of priest and poet
> which was such an important concept to him.
>
> p. 114

Throughout his poetry, Milton combined the classical and biblical allusions. In "Lycidas," the use of the shepherd as a poet is important because the speaker wishes to memorialize a friend in verse which will last forever; the use of the shepherd as a priest in the poem is significant because the speaker learns to celebrate Lycidas' immortality as a foreshadowing of his own. Don Cameron Allen's The Harmonious Vision argues explicitly that Milton was aware of the similarities of these two pastoral traditions and that it would be reasonable to assume that he used them deliberately in "Lycidas" to create his speaker as a shepherd-poet-priest.[17]

Insofar as the speaker's experience of devotion in the poem is concerned, his role as priest takes precedence over his function as poet. Let me follow Arthur Barker's helpful tripartite division of the structure of "Lycidas" in "The Pattern of Milton's 'Nativity Ode.' " Barker divides "Lycidas" as follows: the first "movement" (lines 1-84) laments the shepherd as poet; the second movement (lines 85-131) laments him as priest; and the third movement (lines 132-93) unites these two laments in an apotheosis at the marriage supper of the Lamb.[18] Based on our understanding of Barker's structural analysis of the poem, let me focus specifically on the shepherd-swain as priest. Rosemond Tuve, even though she is not discussing devotion in "Lycidas," but rather the poem's themes and images, notes the poem's principle of devotion in this statement:

> The poem ["Lycidas"] is a tribute, is like some but not
> all elegies in that it is not an object but an act, offered, and
> speaking allegiance . . . [19]

The poem is an "act," an "offering" by one person in memory of another; it works through grief and sorrow to hope by the progress through its materials. Just as Edward King's death is the occasion of Milton's writing "Lycidas," so too the lament itself is an occasion for the speaker within the poem to experience devotion as his sorrow gives way to hope.

Barker understands the first section of the poem to describe Lycidas and the speaker as poets. It is certainly true that the weight of the pastoral materials at the beginning of the poem relate to the swains as poets. They sang as the satyrs danced; even "old Damaetas lov'd to hear [their] Song." The emphasis is on singing -- creative composition -- not the husbandry of the flocks. It is interesting to note that it is the shepherds -- the poets -- who miss Lycidas (l. 49), not the "sheep" at this point in the poem. Of course the important allusion to Orpheus' death emphasizes the loss of Lycidas as a poet rather than as a priest. The first movement of the poem, then, establishes the important subject of immortality, the poet memorializing Lycidas in his poem.

But Milton does not ignore the shepherd's responsibility as priest altogether in this section. The speaker notes that he and Lycidas "fed the same flock" (l. 24) and batt'n[ed their] flocks with the fresh dew of night" while they sang (l. 29). The picture of the shepherds tending the sheep is conventional no doubt, but the speaker makes much later in the poem of the faithless "shepherds" who do not feed their "flocks"; these early references to the pastoral care of the sheep, therefore, take on significance in the light of the section of the poem that presents the shepherd more directly as priest.

In the second section of the poem, according to Barker, the speaker laments Lycidas as a priest. The poet makes little more of the classical pastoral tradition in this section than a list of appropriate references (ll. 85-102). The focus of this second section is the speaker's allusion to Peter:

> Last came and last did go
> The Pilot of the Galilean Lake.
>
> ll. 108-09

In the Gospels, Peter was both a fisherman and "shepherd." By trade, of course, he was a fisherman who worked the Sea of Galilee[20] -- hence Milton's allusion to him here. Peter is invoked, therefore, partly because his vocation makes him an appropriate Christian allusion in an incident of drowning. In addition, the biblical Peter is a shepherd-priest in the New

Testament, in that he has the pastoral responsibility for a "flock" of people: Christ commands Peter three times to "feed [His] sheep,"[21] and Peter eventually spends the rest of his life doing so, as the Book of Acts indicates. It is significant too that Peter was an author of two New Testament epistles. He is an appropriate choice on Milton's part for the first Christian allusion in "Lycidas": as fisherman, he would understand the reality of death by drowning; as shepherd-pastor, he would lament the loss of a "sheep"; as author, he would experience the desire to write. Therefore, Peter provides a suitable link between Christian and classical motifs in the poem, and he emphasizes the shift from poet to priest.

Milton develops only one of Peter's roles at this point in "Lycidas," that of the priest. Milton uses Peter to condemn the corrupt English clergy for not "feeding" their "sheep," namely the English people. Peter eulogizes Lycidas at this point in the poem and laments his death most because he was a "good shepherd" -- one of the few in England at the time. The rest of this section is a bitter diatribe against the faithless religious leaders of Milton's day:

> But the hungry Sheep look up, and are not fed,
> But swoln with wind, and the rank mist they draw,
> Rot inwardly, and foul contagion spread:
> Besides what the grim Wolf with privy paw
> Daily devours apace, and nothing said.
>
> ll. 125-29

This is the bleakest scene of the poem in regards to the speaker's experience of devotion. As a priest who is to celebrate God's goodness, he looks one way and sees a "good shepherd" taken in his prime; he looks the other and sees the "wolves" and "hirelings" (of John 10) fattening themselves at the expense of the people -- "they are sped," the speaker ejaculates (l. 22). Lycidas' death is bad enough in itself, but it is made worse because his place will be filled by a faithless "wolf." Surely the speaker questions God's love here. Either God is not omnipotent and was, therefore, unable to prevent Lycidas' death (and, if this is the case, why worship Him?), or He is uncaring enough to allow a death that He could have prevented -- and should have averted, according to Peter's sharp rebuke of those priests left behind. The emotion here is not despair; it is doubt, doubt in God whom the speaker serves as priest as well as poet. The emotion is paralyzing for the speaker at this point in the poem; all he can do is invoke divine justice, in the form of the "two-handed engine," upon the hireling priests.

The third movement of the poem, according to Barker, synthesizes the two roles of the swain as poet and as priest in an apotheosis of immortality. This section is comprised of a catalogue of flowers, the statement of immortality through Christ, and the promise of tomorrow for the poet-speaker. This section significantly changes the experience of hope that the speaker has and, thereby, provides a valid experience of devotion toward God in the face of that most terrible reminder of sin, death.

The catalogue of flowers provides a modicum of hope to the speaker. Wayne Shumaker's article, "The Archetypal Pattern of Death and Rebirth in 'Lycidas,' " suggests that the flowers in this catalogue become "brightened" and encouraging rather than "somber" and discouraging as they had been earlier in the poem. The "Bells and Flowrets," the speaker tell us in "Lycidas," "are of a thousand hues" (l. 135). Shumaker states, "The result [of this list] is that the grief, while remaining grief, is lifted and brightened."[22] There is a note of optimism on the speaker's part as he describes these flowers.

There is a second reason why the catalogue of flowers which begins the last section of the poem is a source of tentative hope for the speaker. These flowers symbolize a generic "resurrection": that is, because the flowers reproduce themselves in their seeds, they achieve a type of immortality for the species -- a generic immortality. This immortality suggested by the flowers is a symbolic one in that the poet-speaker of the elegy provides a "resurrection" for Lycidas by writing the poem for him.

The speaker is, symbolically at least, the progeny of Lycidas as a poet, thereby providing a "generic" immortality for him: Lycidas' "immortality," or "resurrection," in the speaker also provides the speaker a hope for the same kind of generic resurrection when he should die in the person of another poet who will lament his death.

Even this consolation, however, is not enough. Lycidas is still dead; his "resurrection" is only symbolic and, therefore, impersonal. The catalogue of flowers from the classical tradition of the pastoral elegy is finally inadequate to provide a hope that will overcome the grief that attends the death of an individual person. Therefore, the speaker returns to the Christian tradition to find an adequate hope. He finds that hope specifically in Christ's power over the waves; it is a hope in a personal resurrection for Lycidas, and therefore for himself as well, that he finds in the penultimate verse paragraph of the poem. "Weep no more, woeful Shepherds, weep no more," the speaker begins, "For Lycidas your sorrow is not dead, / Sunk though he be beneath the wat'ry floor" (ll. 165-66). There is life after death --resurrection for the individual-- in these lines. The speaker is confident, even certain, that Lycidas lives. He lives, not only in a general sense in the lines of the speaker of this poem, but in a more particular and personal manner because he attends the "unexpressive nuptial Song" of Revelation 19:9 to which all the saints of all ages are invited. Furthermore, he intercedes, as the "the Genius of the shore," on behalf of all who travel the sea. Both of these references suggest that Lycidas will retain his individuality and personality after death; the speaker is assured of this. If Lycidas has a personal resurrection, then there is hope that the speaker will also have a personal resurrection. This is the hope that "Lycidas" celebrates -- the poet-speaker's assurance of his own, personal immortality.

But on what basis is this type of hope guaranteed? How is this hope a devotional hope? With these questions, we come to the center of the speaker's experience of devotion in the poem. The climactic lines are these:

> So Lycidas, sunk low, but mounted high,
> Through the dear might of him that walk'd
> > the waves,
> Where other groves, and other streams along,
> With Nectar pure his oozy Locks he laves,
> And hears the unexpressive nuptial Song,
> In the blest Kingdoms meek of joy and love.
> > > ll. 172-77

Peter gives way to Christ as the one who provides the basis for hope in resurrection. Peter condemned the faithless shepherds in this poem, and it was Peter who walked on the water with Christ for a brief time. He could not remain on the water, of course, and Christ had to save him as he sank. Just as Christ rescued Peter, so will He resurrect Lycidas as an individual who will attend the "nuptial Song" of the Lamb. It is Christ who assures the speaker of his final victory over death in the poem. Just as the speaker's hope for redemption in the "Nativity Ode" is guaranteed by the incarnation, so too the speaker's hope for his own resurrection in "Lycidas" is assured by the resurrection of Lycidas by Christ's might.

With the speaker's hope having been assured, Milton completes the poem in the final verse paragraph. He promises that the poet-speaker will carry on: "At last he [the speaker] rose, and twich't his Mantle blue: / Tomorrow to fresh Woods, and Pastures new." Here is where Tillyard's statement that Milton, not Edward King, is the subject of "Lycidas" is most helpful: just as the speaker of the poem will write again on the basis of his experience, so too will Milton. As Don Cameron Allen writes in The Harmonious Vision, "The melic [preparatory] period is ended [with "Lycidas"]; there is renewed confidence for the greater task" (p. 56). Milton successfully integrates the development of the speaker from the doubts with which he first faces Lycidas' death to the devout hope with which he will face his own death. This success re-assures him when he writes Paradise Lost so many years later.

Notes
Chapter Two

[1]Hill, pp. 53-54. "English poetry" is to be distinguished from "Latin poetry," the distinction which Milton is making at this point in "At a Vacation Exercise."

[2]Rosemond Tuve, "The Hymn on the Morning of Christ's Nativity," Images and Themes in Five Poems by Milton (Cambridge: Harvard University Press, 1957), pp. 42-43. All subsequent references to this work will be cited in the text in the book.

[3]For example, Isaiah 9:7. "Of the increase of his government and peace there shall be no end, upon the throne of David . . . forever."
And, Isaiah 7:14. "Therefore the Lord himself shall give you a sign; Behold, a virgin shall conceive, and bear a son, and shall call his name Immanuel."

[4]Margaret Drabble, ed., The Oxford Companion to English Literature 5th ed. (Oxford: Clarendon Press, 1986), p. 1140.

[5]Donald M. Rosenberg, Oaten Reeds and Trumpets: Pastoral and Epic in Virgil, Spenser and Milton (East Brunswick, New Jersey: Bucknell University Press, 1981), p. 265.

[6]cf. Paradise Lost, XII, ll. 408-09:

> Proclaiming Life to all who shall believe
> In his redemption . . .

[7]Hanford, p. 154.

[8]cf. Leviticus 17:11. "For the life of the flesh is in the blood: and I have given it to you upon the altar to make an atonement for your souls: for it is the blood that maketh atonement for the soul."
And Hebrews 9:22. "And almost all things are by the law purged with blood; and without the shedding of blood is no remission."

[9]Rosemond Tuve, "Image, Form and Theme in 'A Mask'," Images and Themes in Five Poems by Milton (Cambridge: Harvard University Press, 1962), p. 121.

[10]And also E.M.W. Tillyard, Studies in Milton (London: Chatto and Windus, 1951), pp. 82-99.

[11]Mary Ann Radzinowicz, Toward "Samson Agonistes": The Growth of Milton's Mind (Princeton: Princeton University Press, 1978), p. 347. All subsequent references to this work will be cited in the text of the book.

[12]I have taken the material on the classical heritage of the pastoral elegy tradition which this paragraph presents from Hanford.

[13]C.A. Patrides, ed., Milton's "Lycidas": The Tradition and the Poem (New York: Holt, Rinehart, Winston, 1961), p. 56.

[14]John Crowe Ransom, "A Poem Nearly Anonymous" in C. A. Patrides, ed., Milton's "Lycidas": The Tradition and The Poem (New York: Holt, Rinehart, Winston, 1961), p. 66.

[15]Richard P. Adams, "The Archetypal Pattern of Death and Rebirth in 'Lycidas'," in C. A. Patrides, ed., Milton's "Lycidas": The Tradition and the Poem (New York: Holt, Rinehart, Winston, 1961), pp. 123-24.

[16]E.M.W. Tillyard, "Milton" in C. A. Patrides, ed., Milton's "Lycidas": The Tradition and the Poem. (New York: Holt, Rinehart, Winston, 1961), pp. 123-24.

[17]Don Cameron Allen, The Harmonious Vision: Studies in Milton's Poetry (Baltimore: John Hopkins Press, 1954), pp. 56-57. All subsequent references to this work will be cited in the text of the book.

[18]Arthur Barker, The Pattern of Milton's 'Nativity Ode'," University of Toronto Quarterly, x (1941), pp. 167-81.

[19]Rosemond Tuve, "Theme, Pattern and Imagery in 'Lycidas' " in C. A. Patrides, ed., Milton's "Lycidas": The Tradition and the Poem (New York: Holt, Rinehart, Winston, 1961), p. 129.

[20]cf. Matthew 4:18.

[21]cf. John 21:15-17.

[22]Wayne Shumaker, "Flowerets and Sounding Seas: A Study in the Affective Structure of 'Lycidas' " in C. A. Patrides, ed., Milton's "Lycidas": The Tradition and the Poem (New York: Holt, Rinehart, Winston, 1961), p. 129.

CHAPTER THREE
Paradise Lost

After the publication of "Lycidas" and the completion of his poetic apprenticeship, thirty years elapsed before Milton first published Paradise Lost in 1667. The interval of time was taken up in part by the writing of the prose tracts of the 1640's when Milton thought he saw his religious hopes for God's kingdom in England beginning to be realized and by the writing of The Christian Doctrine in the 1650's.[1] Milton's personal life was in turmoil during these years: he was blind by 1652; and he lost two family members in that same year. In 1660, the Restoration of Charles II dashed all of Milton's hopes for an earthly kingdom of God in England and threatened his personal safety. Once the immediate danger had passed, Milton returned to a more private life and, in the next eleven years, wrote his three most important poems: Paradise Lost, Paradise Regained and Samson Agonistes.

Paradise Lost is the first of Milton's great mature poems. It is both a theodicy and a devotion. As a theodicy, it considers sin, its effects upon men, and God's grace which overcomes the results of sin in men's lives. As a devotion, Paradise Lost presents man's responses to God before and after the fall and demonstrates how the presence of sin in Adam and Eve's experience necessitates their conscious worship of God if they are not to despair of God's love altogether. As John Holloway states, Paradise Lost is a "present rule of life, an insight into how postlapsarian man must face a fallen world, and his own fallen nature."[2] Adam and Eve gain this "insight" as they mature in their expressions of devotion to God and as they experience God's love from them even after the fall. In Paradise Lost, Milton "justif[ies] the ways of God to men" (I. l. 26) by having Adam and

Eve consciously develop their devotion to God, thereby increasing their understanding of God's providence.

The fall of Adam and Eve in Book Nine is the crisis of <u>Paradise Lost</u> and divides the experience of devotion in the poem into two major sections. Books One through Eight give the account of the events in heaven before the creation of the world, the fall of Satan, the creation itself, and the joys of human innocence in the garden of Eden before the fall. In these eight books, Adam and Eve are still sinless; they live in a prelapsarian world until Book Nine. Adam and Eve focus their devotion, therefore, on God as their creator and the giver of the many blessings of Eden. Their devotion is spontaneous and always acceptable to God.

Adam and Eve are not the only ones in this section of the poem to experience devotion to God; the Son and the angels who remain loyal to God also express devotion to the Father in these books. The perspective of both the Son and the loyal angels is always one of sinlessness and purity; moreover, they understand God's ways more completely than do Adam and Eve. Therefore their devotion focuses on more than God's creative activity; it extends to God's future offer of grace to man after his fall. In addition to the Son and the angels in heaven, of course, there is Satan with his host of fallen angels in hell. Because their purpose is "To wage by force or guile eternal War / Irreconcilable to [their] grand Foe [God]" (I, ll. 121-22), however, they clearly do not worship God at all.

In the first section of <u>Paradise Lost</u>, from Book One to Book Eight, we have these perspectives in regard to the subject of devotion: Adam and Eve are sinless and worship God with no restraints; Christ and the loyal angels worship God with a greater knowledge than do Adam and Eve, though they are by no means omniscient; and Satan remains entirely outside of the experience of devotion, his fall already having been completed before the poem begins.

The second major section of <u>Paradise Lost</u>, Books Nine through Twelve, provides the account of the fall of man, its effects on nature, and Michael's chronicle of human history up to the second advent of Christ at the end of time. Adam and Eve's perspective is radically altered by their sinfulness in these books. Ironically, they have an augmented, not a diminished, basis on which to worship God after their fall; God is not only their creator, but, in response to their sin, He becomes their redeemer as well. There is therefore a <u>felix culpa</u> motif at work in the postlapsarian devotional experience of Adam and Eve that makes their devotion more valid for the reader (who is fallen, in Milton's view). In <u>The Christian Poet in "Paradise Lost"</u>, William G. Riggs notes this effect of the fall: "The fall . . . increased man's need for direct manifestations of God's grace" (l. 63). Adam and Eve's devotion matures after the fall because it must if God's providence is to be justified to fallen men.

Even though the Son does not fall into sin with Adam and Eve, His experience of devotion is also deepened by their fall. His obedience to His role in the Father's plan of redemption becomes more immediate and more plain to Him; His choice to obey is a mature one. This is not to say that a simple division of <u>Paradise Lost</u> into two sections accounts for the devotion in the poem. William Riggs warns us not to make too sharp a distinction between prelapsarian and postlapsarian states if we wish to understand Milton's use of the fall and his depiction of Eden. Riggs writes:

> it is only by insisting on a sharp demarcation between fallen and unfallen states that difficulties arise in interpreting the so-called fortunate fall. If we are determined to consider paradise as a static, mindless holiday resort, it is hard to escape the feeling that sin has delivered man into a condition which more adequately challenges his native abilities.
>
> p. 51

Eden is not static -- not for Milton nor for his characters. The fall, therefore, provides more of a crisis than a "sharp demarcation" in the poem in regard to the devotional experiences; the narrative continues in the last four books, though irrevocably altered.

There are two other perspectives on the experiences of devotion in Paradise Lost which we must mention briefly. They are the poet-speaker's and the reader's. Both the speaker and the reader are fallen, sinful. Both are in need of God's grace; both are in need of "inspiration" to understand events from a divine perspective. This is why the poet asks for divine inspiration in his invocations in Books One, Three, Seven and Nine. And, this is why the reader must read the poem. Only a fallen man needs to read a theodicy; the unfallen man understands God's ways "immediately" -- without a mediator. Speaker and reader, therefore, are in a position to learn that mature devotion is active and willingly given, just as Adam and Eve come to learn after their fall.

For Milton, freedom of will is essential to devotion. It is essential both to prelapsarian and postlapsarian men. Free will is active in Milton's view. Man is not "predestinated" fatalistically to a predetermined action; in regards to salvation, for instance, Milton rejects the idea of "reprobation," or the fore-ordained damnation of some men to hell.[3] Man is truly free to choose, else God's ways are unjustifiable and man's devotion to God is slavery, not love. Milton is clear on this issue in Areopagitica:

> Many there be that complain of divine providence for suffering Adam to transgress. Foolish tongues! when God gave him reason, he gave him freedom to choose, for reason is but choosing; he had been else a mere artificial Adam, such an Adam as he is in the motions. We ourselves esteem not of that obedience, or love, or gift, which is of force. God therefore left him free, set before him a provoking object, ever almost in his eyes; herein consisted his merit, herein the right of his reward, the praise of his abstinence. Wherefore did he create passions within us, pleasures round about us,

but that these rightly tempered are the very ingredient of virtue?

p. 733

God allowed man the freedom to choose to serve Him; He did not coerce that service. In John Milton: Poet, Priest and Prophet, John Spencer Hill defines Milton's concept of free will as the legitimate choice "to grow either toward God or away from Him" (p. 120). To grow away from God is sin; to grow toward God is devotion. Devotion is the active exercise of man's free will to "grow toward God."

Adam and Eve in both their prelapsarian and postlapsarian states are free to worship and serve God. The fall does not introduce free will to man in Milton's view; rather, man was created originally with the ability to choose to obey or disobey God. In Milton's view, devotion must be expressed willingly. John Hill notes that there is always choice facing Milton's Adam and Eve: before the fall, their choice is between "known good and potential evil"; after the fall, the choice is between "known good and known evil" (p. 120). The difference is not that there is choice only after the fall, but that the choice involves "known evil" after the fall as opposed to "potential evil" before the fall.[4] In both contexts, Adam and Eve can worship God willingly -- or disobey Him willfully. J. M. Evans emphasizes the same crucial point in "Paradise Lost" and the Genesis Tradition. He refutes the position of Willey and Waldock that Adam and Eve's prelapsarian innocence is "effortless," and argues instead that they must maintain a "constant vigilance" if they are to retain their innocence at all. Their innocent prelapsarian state is "conditional," Evans asserts -- conditional upon their obedience.[5] And they are free to disobey, if they choose. Therefore, devotion in Paradise Lost is predicated on Milton's insistence that man has a valid free will to choose to express devotion to God -- or not -- as he wishes.

But free will involves more than external alternatives to choose from; it involves "self-knowledge" as well. To be free, we must know not only what the choices are, but which one is best for us. This is where Adam and Eve fail; Eve assesses her situation incorrectly and determines that disobedience to God's stricture on the tree of the knowledge of good and evil is her best course of action. She rationalizes:

> Here grows the Cure of all, this Fruit Divine,
> Fair to the Eye, inviting to the Taste,
> Of virtue to make wise.
>
> IX, ll. 776-78

Eve lacks self-knowledge; at least, she lacks proper self-knowledge as Hill defines it. "Self-knowledge" for Milton, Hill argues, is "knowledge of self in God and in relation to God" (p. 121). Eve chooses knowledge of herself apart from God, not in God; Adam willfully chooses to follow Eve. Devotion in Paradise Lost, therefore, is predicated on the development of proper self-knowledge -- "knowledge of self in God," as well as on freedom of will. The two factors provide a paradox: Adam and Eve have freedom of will to reject God, but it is only by acknowledging God that they are free -- free to know themselves.

I have stated that Adam and Eve's experience of devotion in Paradise Lost is influenced greatly by the presence of sin. Milton writes three of the twelve books of Paradise Lost before Adam and Eve appear and speak. It is not until Book Four that the reader sees Adam and Eve, and that through Satan's envious eyes:

> Two of far nobler shape erect and tall,
> Godlike erect with native Honor clad
> In naked Majesty seem'd Lords of all.
>
> IV, ll. 288-90

Adam does not speak for another one hundred lines. When he does, he offers a hymn of praise to God as his creator, "infinitely good" (l. 413). Before the appearance of Adam and Eve in their Edenic joy, however, the poet has narrated a vast background of events in heaven and hell that provide an ironic context for the picture of the innocent Adam and Eve. The first two books present Satan, fallen from his glory as Lucifer, the champion of sin in the universe; almost half of the third book accounts for Satan's activities as well. Only the first four hundred lines of Book Three present the scene in heaven and the characters of the Father, the Son and the unfallen angels. Before Adam and Eve speak at all, therefore, the reader is aware of the cosmological warfare that has preceded creation and the awesome magnitude of their arch-enemy, Satan. The first devotional speech in the poem is, appropriately, Christ's reaction to the Father's intent to provide a solution to man's sin by His grace.

At the council in heaven in Book Three, the Father announces His plan to extend mercy to Adam and Eve when they sin:

> Man falls deceiv'd
> By th'other first: Man therefore shall find grace,
> The other none: in Mercy and Justice both,
> Through Heav'n and Earth, so shall my glory excel,
> But Mercy first and last shall brightest shine.
>
> III, ll. 130-34

This is "prevenient" grace, grace that foresees (not foreordains) man's fall and reverses the effects of sin by providing mercy.

Apparently, the Son first learns of the Father's plan for offering grace to fallen men from this announcement. The Father has the role of authority in the interchange with the Son about grace in Book Three. He announces grace as a fait accompli; the Son responds with praise for God's mercy:

> O Father, gracious was the word which clos'd
> Thy sovran sentence, that Man should find grace;

> For which both Heav'n and Earth shall high extol
> Thy praises. . .

III, ll. 144-47a

Already in this speech the Son displays His earnest care for man that he should not be cast off by God forever -- "that be from thee far, / That be far from thee, Father," Christ exclaims in the same speech (ll. 153-54). He is grateful that the Father, in His prescience, has provided a solution to man's future sin. In The Christian Doctrine, Milton defines gratitude as that attitude "whereby we acknowledge [God's] goodness in conferring benefits upon creatures so unworthy as [men]" (CI, XVII, p. 59). Christ is grateful on man's behalf even before he sins. This is a clear definition of grace, as well as of gratitude: grace is God's free "benefits" to "unworthy" men who deserve punishment, not mercy, for their sin.

Christ's experience of gratitude here, however, is not the reader's. Christ learns of the Father's offer of grace from his dialogue with the Father in Book Three. The reader, on the other hand, already knows from the biblical account that Christ's crucifixion and resurrection are necessary for man to realize God's grace. The reader, then, is privy to information which the Son does not know at this point in the narrative. In John Milton: Poet, Priest and Prophet, John Spencer Hill admonishes us to be careful to distinguish between our perspective as readers and Christ's as the agent of man's future redemption in this section of the poem. If we are not alert here, Hill warns, we will "run the risk of serious misinterpretation, either by ascribing to the Son a prescience which (for Milton) he does not possess or, more grievously, by interpreting the Atonement offer as a pre-arranged scenario between the Father and the Son" (pp. 123-24). The "devout affection" of gratitude on Christ's part for the Father's announcement of His offer of grace to men is more important in the development of the Son's devotional experience than it is to the reader's at this point in the poem.

Gratitude is not the only devotional reaction that is prompted by the Father's announcement of His intention to extend grace to man. The Son also expresses His intent to be obedient to the Father in carrying out His responsibilities so that man can receive grace. Because man will be sinful, he cannot atone for himself: "Atonement for himself or offering meet," the Son tells us, "Indebted and undone, [man] hath none to bring" (III, ll 234-35). Therefore, the sinless Son offers to expiate man's sin. He says to the Father:

> Behold mee then, mee for him, life for life
> I offer, on mee let thine anger fall;
> Account mee man.
>
> III, ll. 236-38a

Christ's obedience extends to His willingness to be separated from God and to die on the cross to "lead Hell captive maugre Hell" (III, l. 255). Milton's definition of obedience as one of the devout affections in The Christian Doctrine applies perfectly to the Son's attitude in this speech. Milton defines obedience as "that virtue whereby we propose to ourselves the will of God as the paramount rule of our conduct" (CE, XVII, p. 69). Even Christ obeys God; here, as elsewhere, obedience comes from the free will of the one who obeys. Thus, at the announcement of divine grace, Christ shows both gratitude and obedience to God the Father, even before man has fallen into sin. The significance of the Son's devotional expressions is that He develops a stronger commitment to the Father from having heard His offer of mercy to men. Christ moves from gratitude to obedience in Book Three; He intends to offer His life for man's life.

The Son is not the only one to praise God in gratitude for His plan to redeem fallen man by grace. The loyal angels sing an extended hymn of praise, first to the Father and then to the Son for loving man enough to die in order for God to extend grace to fallen man. The speaker reports the angels' praise of God as the Father of creation:

> Thee Father first they sung Omnipotent,
> Immutable, Immortal, Infinite,

Eternal King; thee Author of all being.

III, ll. 372-74

The angels celebrate God and magnify Him by naming His attributes, but modulate their praise quickly toward the Son:

> Thee next they sang of all Creation first,
> Begotten Son, Divine Similitude,
> In whose conspicious count'nance, without cloud
> Made visible, th'Almighty Father shines.

III, ll. 363-86

These verses suggest Milton's mature anti-Trinitarian theology. If Christ was created, His nature and "lifespan" are not divine in the same way as the Father's are. If Christ is not God in Milton's view in <u>Paradise Lost</u>, His speeches of petition, gratitude and obedience all become profoundly devotional as the attitudes of a created being toward God. Even the angels regard the Son to be of a different essence than the Father when they note that "No sooner did [the Son] / Perceive [God] purpos'd not to doom frail Man" (III, ll. 403-04), than He offered to redeem him. The Son is not omniscient if He must learn what the Father already knows. At the very least, Christ's dual nature as God and man allows his humanity to express devotion to God the Father, even in heaven before the fall. The angels in heaven echo the Son's praise to the Father and suggest a pattern for Adam and Eve to follow. As they are superior to men and yet still worship the Father, so Adam and Eve should worship Him, too. All that the Son and the angels celebrate about God in Book Three is His creation of man and His projected plan to redeem him.

When in Book Six God plans to defeat Satan and his rebel host, the Son develops His obedience to the Father yet further than he does in Book Three. After God gives Christ the mandate to subdue Satan, the Son responds in complete commitment to the task, finding personal glory only insofar as He "exalts" the Father:

O Father, O Supreme of heav'nly Thrones,
First, Highest, Holiest, Best, thou always seek'st
To glorify thy Son, I always thee,
As is most just; this I my Glory account
My exaltation, and my whole delight,
That thou in me well pleas'd, declar'st thy will
Fulfill'd, which to fulfill is all my bliss.

VI, ll. 723-29

Milton's emphasis in this speech is not so much on the divinity of the Son as on His obedience to the Father, for He makes "the will of God the paramount rule of [His] conduct" (CE, XVII, p. 69). He wishes to "fulfill" the Father's will; this is "all [His] bliss." Of course, the Father's will here is for the imprisonment of Satan in the lake of fire. Therefore, the Son states, "Whom thou hat'st, I hate, and put on / Thy terrors, as I put thy mildness on." He will crush Satan where Michael and Gabriel could not. The result of Christ's defeat of Satan, however, is not praise of himself, but praise to the Father alone. Christ announces that "all thy Saints unmixt" shall "Unfeigned Halleluiahs to thee [God] sing, / Hymns of high praise, and I among them chief" (VI, ll. 744-45). Here again Milton depicts Christ, even before the creation and fall of man, offering devotion to God for His grace toward man and judgment of Satan. Before the fall, Christ and the angels offer God their gratitude and their obedience in relation to His grace to be offered to fallen men; what is more, Christ develops a more complete obedience to God between Book Three and Book Six.

Though there is the devotion to the Father which we have noted on the parts of the Son and the loyal angels before the fall, it is Adam's and Eve's expressions of devotion that are most fully developed by the poet. Adam and Eve appear in the poem for the first time in Book Four and, until the end of Book Eight, they experience devotion for God in a prelapsarian condition. In this sinless state, the first parents express devotion to God as their creator -- often in hymns of praise that are not yet affected by the presence of sin. With their fall in Book Nine, however, Adam and Eve must first repent of their sin and learn to worship God not only as their creator, but also as their redeemer. Devotion in the last four books of the poem, therefore, tends to be less spontaneous than it is in the first eight books when Adam and Eve are innocent.

The predominant devotion in the first eight books of Paradise Lost is Adam and Eve's celebration of God as their creator and provider. They express their love to God before the fall in their innocent gratitude and obedience; these are the major motivations of their devotion. Even in prelapsarian Eden, devotion is a conscious and an active expression of love to God. There is even an underlying irony in Adam's first speech in the poem. It is a devotional speech, but it is overheard by Satan who has just arrived in Eden to learn how best to deceive Adam and Eve into sin. The scene presents the reader with the first actual appearance of Adam and Eve in the narrative and gives us Adam's and Eve's first speeches. The scene is ironic in that we see our first parents when Satan sees them. Satan is filled with envy and jealousy at the sight of the happiness of Adam and Eve (IV, ll. 501-03). Adam and Eve speak in perfect innocence of evil, even of the threat of evil which is so close to them at this early point in the narrative. The irony of the reader's perspective emphasizes the beauty of the love which Adam and Eve express for God.

Adam's first speech to Eve is an exhortation to gratitude and obedience for God's beneficence toward them. He begins by praising God for His goodness (an important motivation for Adam's love throughout the poem):

> Sole partner and sole part of these joys,
> Dearer thyself than all; needs must the Power
> That made us, and for us this ample World
> Be infinitely good, and of his good
> As liberal and free as infinite,
> That rais'd us from the dust and plac't us here

In all this happiness, who at his hand
Have nothing merited, nor can perform
Aught whereof he hath need.

IV, ll. 411-19a

The bounty and beauty of the garden of Eden elicit Adam's devotion to God. He is grateful for God's "liberality" in providing "this ample World," for God's generosity attests to His goodness. In The Paradise Within, Louis L. Martz speaks of Adam's gratitude as an "intuitive movement toward the love of God" (p. 132). God's love, as evidenced in His ample provision for Adam and Eve's happiness in Eden, prompts Adam's loving gratitude. More than this, this first speech provides us with a hint of grace, too: Adam and Eve "have nothing merited" God's love. Even though it is addressed to Eve, Adam's first reaction to God is one of gratitude for "His goodness" to "creatures so unworthy" as himself (CE, XVII, p. 59).

The devout affection which most readily accompanies gratitude toward God is obedience to His commands. After all, Adam argues, God has placed only one stricture upon him and Eve among the many blessings which He has conferred upon them. It is only reasonable, therefore, to obey that one command. Adam says to Eve:

hee who requires
From us no other service than to keep
This one, this easy charge, of all the Trees
In paradise that bear delicious fruit
So various, not to taste that only Tree
Of Knowledge, planted by the Tree of Life.

IV, ll. 419b-24

The command "not to taste that only Tree / Of knowledge" is "the only sign of our obedience left," Adam argues (IV, ll. 423-24, 428). In the prelapsarian state, gratitude is not an inadequate motive for Adam and Eve's obedience. Without sin, Adam has no need of God's grace;

therefore, all that he experiences of God is his love for Him as his creator. Adam's devotional attitudes of gratitude and obedience are proper responses to God. He summarizes his devotion as he concludes his speech to Eve:

> let us ever praise him, and extol
> His bounty, following our delightful task
> To prune these growing Plants, and tend these
> Flow'rs,
> Which were it toilsome, yet with thee were sweet.
>
> IV, ll. 436-39

Adam's exhortation is to serve God; in Eden before the fall, this service is rendered by Adam and Eve's cultivating the garden as God commanded. Again, obedience is active: Adam is, on the one hand, to avoid the tree of the knowledge of good and evil and, on the other hand, to "prune these growing Plants." Obedience demonstrates gratitude.

When Eve replies to Adam's speech regarding God, she does so in prelapsarian innocence which shows perfect satisfaction with the lot that God has given her:

> O thou for whom
> And from whom I was form'd flesh of thy flesh,
> And without whom am to no end, my Guide
> And Head, what thou hast said is just and right.
> For wee to him indeed all praises owe,
> And daily thanks.
>
> IV, ll. 440-45

Eve accepts her position under Adam and God without question and worships God accordingly. Adam is her "guide" and "head." Adam's exhortation to worship God is enough reason for Eve to do so. Of course, at the fall, Eve rebels against what she then perceives as a position of "subservience" to Adam. As Adam obeys God before the fall, however, so

Eve obeys Adam. This is Milton's view of the chain of responsibility before the fall. Adam and Eve obey those responsibilities without question because they are commanded by God. Hence, the first devotion of Adam and Eve in the garden is unalloyed in that no sin interferes with the couple's gratitude and obedience to God and and His ordinances in their lives. Paradoxically, they express their free wills by deliberately choosing God's will that they be grateful and obedient; by obeying God, they realize their fullest potential as humans.

Milton expands Adam and Eve's praise to include the whole of the prelapsarian creation. Adam is not unique in his praise; he is merely the highest of created, earthly beings who render praise to God as their creator. In his devotion to God, Adam is in perfect "harmony" with the universe before the fall. He himself tells us this:

> Millions of spiritual Creatures walk the Earth
> Unseen, both when we wake, and when we sleep:
> All these with ceaseless praise his works behold
> Both day and night; how often from the steep
> Of echoing Hill or Thicket have we heard
> Celestial voices . . .
> Singing their great Creator.
>
> IV, ll. 677-82a, 684a

The universe is in perfect harmony and agreement in its praise to God as its creator. This is the music of the spheres topos, used here to show the universality of "unmediated," prelapsarian praise to God. Adam is only one "note" in that symphony, albeit the highest earthly one. He is fulfilling his proper function in the symphony of creation by teaching Eve to praise God as their creator. All of nature joins in the hymn to God.

Before they retire for their night's rest at this point in the narrative of Book Four, Adam and Eve discuss their perfect bliss. Their dialogue forms a hymn of praise to God for all that He has given them, but especially for each other. Because he is responsible for Eve, Adam begins the hymn, noting that "God hath set / Labor and rest" (IV, ll. 612-13) both in their cycles for man's benefit. He recognizes that God's plan that they cultivate Eden is an acknowledgment of their dignity. "Man hath his daily work of body or mind / Appointed," he says to Eve (IV, ll. 618-19). Adam understands that his task is active; even praise in this hymn is a manifestation of that active love.

Eve's response to Adam is an expression of her love not only for Adam, but also for God. She replies to Adam:

> My Author and Disposer, what thou bidd'st
> Unargu'd I obey; so God ordains,
> God is thy Law, thou mine: to know no more
> Is woman's happiest knowledge and her praise.
>
> IV, ll. 635-38

Eve obeys Adam and submits to know no more than her position allows. We must not let our modern concern with Eve's submission to Adam have us misinterpret the devotion that Eve is expressing in these lines. By recognizing her position in relation to Adam, Eve acknowledges her love for God; her obedience to Adam is love for God. Eve's response to Adam's hymn of praise to God is a hymn of praise of her own -- to Adam and, through him, to God the Father.

Adam concludes his evening hymn with a doxology to the Father for His having created a beautiful world and, more importantly, for His having given him Eve:

> Thou also mad'st the Night,
> Maker Omnipotent, and thou the Day,
> Which we in our appointed work imploy'd
> Have finisht happy in our mutual help

And mutual love, the Crown of all our bliss
Ordain'd by thee.

IV, ll. 724-29a

Adam's final speech on the first day that we see him is a hymn of gratitude to God for Eden, for the cycle of the daytime work and nighttime rest, and for Eve's "help" and "love." Adam's gratitude for Eve, however, is the focus of his doxology to God. There is nothing lustful or selfish in Adam and Eve's prelapsarian enjoyment of their mutual love. Their pleasure in love before the fall is a perfectly legitimate expression of their love for God; they are obeying His mandate to them to "be fruitful and multiply." Hence, Milton expresses love for God, gratitude to Him and obedience through the prelapsarian marriage relationship of Adam and Eve.

It remains for the narrator to comment on Adam and Eve's obedience after Adam expresses their gratitude. The narrator states that the innocent "connubial love" of Adam and Eve is "adoration pure":

but adoration pure
Which God likes best, into thir inmost bower
Handed they went; and eas'd the putting off
These troublesome disguises which wee wear,
Straight side by side were laid, nor turn'd I ween
Adam from his fair Spouse, nor Eve the Rites
Mysterious of connubial Love refus'd.

IV, ll 737b-44

God's command to Adam and Eve to procreate is not burdensome: children will help parents to cultivate the garden and, thereby, obey God. It is not until after the fall, when Eve wishes to remain childless so as to frustrate Satan (X, ll. 979-91), that this command becomes a serious test of obedience. In Book Four, it is still the "Rites / Mysterious of connubial Love" (ll. 743-44).

Though the whole created universe praises God before the fall, Milton is primarily interested in the devotion of Adam and Eve. In Book Five, the poet returns to Adam and Eve, and we hear their morning hymns of God. Gratitude and obedience are important devout affections in the hymns, but here Milton most emphasizes the love that they have toward God. In The Christian Doctrine, Milton defines love as the preference of God "above all other objects of affection" and the desire to bring Him "glory" (CE, XVII, pp. 51 and 53). Adam's gratitude responds to what God has done for him; his obedience comes from what God has commanded him; his love, however, reflects who God is Himself, regardless of the blessings He bestows. The object of Adam's devotional love, therefore, is God Himself.

Immediately before Adam and Eve sing their "orisons" to God, the narrator introduces their hymn this way:

Thir Orisons, each morning duly paid
In various style, for neither various style
Nor holy rapture wanted they to praise
Thir Maker, in fit strains pronounct or sung
Unmeditated, such prompt eloquence
Flow'd from thir lips, in Prose or numerous Verse,
More tuneable than needed Lute or Harp
To add more sweetness, and they thus began.

V, ll. 145-52

The narrator comments on the spontaneity, the "unmeditated" and "prompt" nature of the orisons that Adam and Eve sing to God. Since there is no sin, they sing without restraint. The narrator's emphasis on the spontaneity of their hymns suggests that Adam and Eve freely and naturally focus their attention on God each morning. There is no constraint placed upon them to do so, only their own unforced love.

Adam emphasizes the love he has for God when he sings his hymn of praise, which begins with these words:

> These are thy glorious works, Parent of good,
> Almighty, thine this universal Frame
> Thus wondrous fair; thyself how wondrous then!
> Unspeakable, who sit'st above these Heavens
> To us invisible or dimly seen
> In these thy lowest works, yet these declare
> Thy goodness beyond thought, and Power Divine.
>
> V, ll. 153-59

As he surveys God's "wondrous works" all around him, Adam meditates on God Himself: "thyself how wondrous then," he exclaims. Adam is overwhelmed with the thought of God's wonder, "goodness beyond thought," and His "Power Divine." Meditating on what God has done for them in creating the world for their use, and contemplating what God must be like to have made so many beautiful creatures, Adam can respond only in love: "witness if I be silent, Morn or Even, / To Hill, or Valley, Fountain, or fresh shade / Made vocal by my Song, and taught his praise." He cannot remain silent, he tells us; he must praise God for His great bounty to him. His song, therefore, is one way to glorify God. The primary motivation for Adam's gratitude and obedience is love for God who has done so much for him.

Even in their daytime work in the garden before the fall, Adam and Eve repeatedly sing praises to God. Joseph H. Summers argues in The Muse's Method that the songs which Adam and Eve sing while they cultivate the garden glorify God; they are doxologies which punctuate the work.[6] For instance, all of nature joins Adam in this paeon to the creator:

> Hail universal Lord, be bounteous still
> To give us only good.
>
> V, ll. 205-06

Within one hundred lines of Adam's hymn of praise, Eve comments on God's "bounties" (l. 330) and observes at length the amplitude of Eden: all delicacies from India, "Pontus or the Punic coast" (l. 340); all "must, and meaths / From many a berry," "dulcet creams" with "Rose and Odors from the shrub infus'd" provide pleasure to the innocent pair (V, ll. 333-49). Eve is grateful for them all; or, more exactly, she is grateful that God has provided such abundance in Eden. These little doxologies attest to a consciousness of God's liberality.

Nor is Adam niggardly of what he has received from God in His goodness. When Raphael arrives in Book Five to speak with him about God's creation of him, Adam proffers him a banquet from God's bounty:

> Heav'nly stranger, please to taste
> These bounties which our Nourisher, from whom
> All perfect good unmeasur'd out, descends
> To us for food and for delight hath caus'd
> The Earth to yield; unsavory food perhaps
> To spiritual Natures; only this I know,
> That one Celestial Father gives to all.
>
> V, ll. 397-403

Adam is both generous with his foods and eager to indicate his gratitude to "that one Celestial Father [who] gives to all." These few brief hymns of praise and acknowledgments of gratitude to God on Adam's and Eve's parts during their daily activities attest to the active, omnipresent gratitude that they have in their innocent state for the Father's kindness.

In Books One through Eight, therefore, Milton demonstrates several types of devotion to God. Christ and the angels foreshadow God's grace to fallen men with expressions of gratitude; Christ offers His obedience to God's role for Him in the plan of man's redemption; and Adam and Eve praise God and willingly obey Him for His creating them and then bestowing abundant blessings upon them in each other and in the natural creation. Because they have not yet sinned, however, they cannot express devotion to God for His grace. The worship in the prelapsarian experience of the poem, then, concentrates on God as creator.

In the postlapsarian books of Paradise Lost, on the other hand, devotion does focus mainly on God's grace and His providence in men's lives. The fall of man does not limit the experience of devotion in the poem; rather, it expands it. Whereas in their prelapsarian lives Adam and Eve loved God only as their creator and provider, in their postlapsarian state they learn to love God as their redeemer as well. Their love for God as their creator and provider is not negated in Books Nine through Twelve; this love is increased by their love for God as their redeemer. Because of sin, Adam and Eve lose their immediate -- non-mediated -- communication with God and must work even more consciously and actively to express devotion to God. In addition, their free will is limited by the fall in that, though they have experienced both evil and good, their ability to choose rightly between them is diminished by sin. But these changes do not nullify devotion in the poem; on the contrary, they necessitate devotion all the more. In Books Nine through Twelve of Paradise Lost, therefore, all of the characters (except the Father, the Son and the loyal angels, of course) are fallen; speaker, reader, and Adam and Eve are all in need of devotion.

The Son provides the hope that sin and death are not final. It is the Son's obedience to His role in the Father's plan of redemption that provides the basis on which Adam and Eve come to understand that the Father has taken their sin into account and that He will reverse its effects for them. The Son asks the Father to allow Him to redeem fallen man:

> See Father, what first fruits on Earth are sprung
> From thy implanted Grace in Man, these Sighs
> And Prayers, which in this Golden Censer, mixt
> With Incense, I thy Priest before thee bring,
> Fruits of more pleasing savor from thy seed

Sown with contrition in his heart, than those
Which his own hand manuring all the Trees
Of Paradise could have produc't, ere fall'n
From innocence. Now therefore bend thine ear
To supplication, hear his sighs though mute;
Unskilful with what words to pray, let mee
Interpret for him, mee his Advocate
And propitiation, all his works on mee
Good or not good ingraft, my Merit those
Shall perfect, and for these my Death shall pay.
Accept me, and in mee from these receive
The smell of peace toward Mankind, let him live
Before thee reconcil'd, at least his days
Number'd, though sad, till Death, his doom
      (which I
To mitigate thus plead, not to reverse)
To better life shall yield him, where with mee
All my redeem'd may dwell in joy and bliss,
Made one with me as I with thee am one.
XI, ll. 22-44

Just as when He created them God gave Adam and Eve the garden of Eden to cultivate and enjoy, so too does He give them His grace for their redemption after they fall.   Like the plants in the garden, grace is "implanted" like a "seed" in man's heart. Adam's contrition is the fertilizer for this seed of God's grace. Just as Adam was to cultivate Eden, so too God "cultivates" grace in Adam's and Eve's hearts and leads them to produce the devotional "fruits" of contrition and gratitude. God is now the gardener, Adam the garden. God's grace and man's penitence form a "more pleasing savor" to God than did Adam's husbandry of the trees and fruits in Eden before the fall. Hope for this future restoration which God's prevenient grace plans for man is to be realized on the basis of the Son's obedience to the Father.

It is to guarantee grace to man <u>after</u> he falls that Milton has Christ ask to be allowed to redeem man in Book Three <u>before</u> man falls. Prevenient grace guarantees redemption and provides Adam and Eve -- and the reader as well -- with the certainty that devotion after the fall is not in vain. In the first council in heaven, the Son says to the Father:

> Behold mee then, mee for him, life for life
> I offer, on mee let thine anger fall;
> Account mee man.
>
> III, ll. 236-38

The Son asks to be the substitute for man -- "on mee let thine anger fall," he asks of the Father -- to take the penalty for man's sin. The Father demonstrates His grace by accepting the Son's offer without reservation:

> thy merit
> Imputed shall absolve them who renounce
> Thir own both righteous and unrighteous deeds,
> And live in thee transplanted, and from thee
> Receive new life.
>
> III, ll. 290-94

The Father will grant sinful man Christ's righteousness ("thy merit / Imputed") and, therefore, be able to accept man once again sinless -- in Christ. Isabel Rivers explains the theology of this transaction in <u>Classical and Christian Ideals in English Renaissance Poetry</u>:

> God's justice, which punishes man for the sin of disobedience, is matched by his mercy, which forgives man. Yet his justice demands satisfaction. This is achieved through the mediation of God's greatest gift to man, his Son, the second Adam, whose perfect obedience cancels the disobedience of the first Adam, and who gives himself as a sacrifice, thereby taking on himself man's sin and redeeming

him from damnation. The disobedience of the first Adam brought man death; the obedience of the second Adam brings man eternal life. Just as Christ takes on man's sin, though he is himself sinless, so he imputes to man his righteousness, though fallen man is himself incapable of righteousness. God accepts Christ's imputed righteousness or merits as man's, and thus grants man salvation.

p. 113

This plan of redemption for fallen man is worked out, and agreed upon, by the Father and the Son in Book Three of <u>Paradise Lost</u> before Adam and Eve fall. Yet in Book Eleven, the Son asks the Father to accept Him as man's "advocate / And propitiation" (XI, ll. 34-35). Christ will both pay man's debt -- this is "propitiation" -- and defend him before God when he sins -- this is His "advocacy." In addition, Christ asks God to "accept [Him], and in [Him] from these receive / The smell of peace toward Mankind" (XI, ll. 37-38).[7] Yet all of this plan was agreed upon before Creation and reported in Book Three. Surely, then, Christ is repeating His obedience to the Father in all of His plan. As Milton defines it, "obedience is that virtue whereby we propose to ourselves the will of God as the paramount rule of our conduct" (CE, XVII, p. 69). Even Christ, therefore, approaches God the Father devotionally after man's fall; He expresses God's will and also obeys it Himself. In Book Three, the reader has seen God's promise that He will redeem man. He has seen Christ's reminder of that promise in Book Eleven. Therefore, he has a certain hope that God will fulfill His promise.

Before the Book Eleven dialogue in heaven between Father and Son takes place in the chronology of Milton's narrative, Adam and Eve have already repented of their sinful disobedience against God's stricture upon their eating of the fruit of the forbidden tree. Adam and Eve realize God's grace after they repent of their sins. At the end of the tenth book, for instance, Adam and Eve pray for forgiveness:

> and there confess
> Humbly our faults, and pardon beg, with tears
> Watering the ground, and with our sighs the Air
> Frequenting, sent from hearts contrite, in sign
> Of sorrow unfeign'd, and humiliation meek.
>
> X, ll. 1088-92

This is one of Adam's most poignant penitential "prayers" in Paradise Lost. It comes after Adam and Eve have both accused each other bitterly for having sinned, and also after they have made an attempt to reconcile themselves to each other. The prayer concludes Book Ten and, in Book Eleven, Michael comes to encourage Adam and Eve with the eschatological victory of God's grace over the serpent. Adam "confesses" his "faults" to God here, and "begs" for "pardon" and forgiveness. The prayer is an informal expression of penitence: penitence admits guilt and seeks pardon. Twice, Adam speaks of his humility as he prays. Adam's humility reverses his earlier "pride against God," as Milton calls it in The Christian Doctrine (CE, XVII, p. 65); rather than asserting his will against God's Adam learns that his most appropriate course of action -- the one in which, paradoxically, he realizes his own identity best -- is to admit guilt and ask forgiveness. Humility is the proper first response to God for Adam after he has sinned. He has loved God for His beneficence to him before the fall. As this point in the narrative, however, he has not yet experienced God's grace in redemption so that humility, rather than love, is Adam's appropriate posture at the end of Book Ten.

At the climax of Michael's narrative of human history in Book Twelve, Milton turns Adam's humility into hope. In a brief forty-six verses, Michael recounts the major events of Christ's death, resurrection, ascension, and second advent which form the basis of the Christian hope of eternal life. The economy of Michael's account intensifies the impact of the climactic events of Christ's incarnate work, especially in the light of the almost leisurely pace of the rest of Michael's chronicle. After Adam hears of the completion of the proto evangelium (that Eve's "seed" would "bruise" the serpent's "head"), he breaks into a spontaneous song of praise, exclaiming:

> O Goodness infinite, goodness immense!
> That all this good of evil shall produce,
> And evil turn to good; more wonderful
> Than that by which creation first brought forth
> Light out of darkness!
>
> XII, ll. 469-73

This is Milton's most important articulation of the <u>felix culpa</u> motif through which he seeks to "justify the ways of God to men" (fallen men, that is). Adam tells us that God's grace in His plan of redemption is "more wonderful" than His beneficence in creation. Adam's hope at this point in the narrative is a clear contrast to his despair after his fall. Earlier he had exclaimed:

> O miserable of happy! is this the end
> Of this new glorious World, and mee so late
> The Glory of that Glory, who now become
> Accurst of blessed, hide me from the face
> Of God, whom to behold was then my highth
> Of happiness.
>
> X, ll.720-25

Whichever way he turns, he seems to find no hope. All is bleak for Adam; he despairs that he will ever be happy again. At this point, he lacks all hope. Adam's hymn in Book Twelve, therefore, is an important example of the devotional attitude of hope, "that by which we expect with certainty the fulfillment of God's promises" (CE, XVII, p. 57). Adam rejoices as if Christ had already completed His role in the plan of redemption; yet all of this is still future at the time of its telling. Surely this is "expecting" with "certainty" the fulfillment of the promise. This is what Milton calls hope and the Bible calls faith. Significantly, the hymn focuses on God's character, specifically His "goodness" (repeated four times in five verses), as all legitimate devotion does in Milton's view. From Adam's perspective, this is the theological climax of <u>Paradise Lost</u>; here he realizes the extent of God's love and grace for him.

Prior to realizing that the Father would turn evil to good, Adam and Eve come to understand that God loves them, not only as the first parents of the human race, but also as individuals. One of Eve's earliest reactions to the fall was to seek to avoid the divine penalty of death which God placed upon her and Adam. But death was not God's only sentence on the sinful pair; He condemned Adam to eat by the sweat of his brow and Eve to bear children in pain (cf. Genesis 3:16-19). Eve proposes to avoid her sentence by dying childless (X, I. 989) She even goes so far as to suggest that she and Adam end their lives immediately so as to ensure her barrenness:

> Let us seek Death, or he not found, supply
> With our own hands his Office on ourselves
> X, II. 1002-03

This is an example of "impatience under the divine decrees" (CE, XVII, p. 67) which Milton cites in <u>The Christian Doctrine</u> as an antithesis to hope. Clearly, Eve wishes to avoid sin's penalty for her progeny, as well as for herself, by committing suicide (cf. X, II. 988-91). It is in response to Eve's despair that Adam gives his most significant devotional speech after the fall. In it, he tries to encourage Eve with the hope of God's promise that He would bruise Satan's head by her seed (X, II. 1028-32). He counsels her to patience, a devout affection which Milton defines as "that [emotion] whereby we acquiesce in the promises of God, through a confident reliance on his divine providence, power and goodness, and bear inevitable evils with equanimity, as the dispensation of the supreme Father, and sent for our good" (CE, XVII, p. 67). Adam's encouragement of Eve is an example of this kind of patience, which is an active patience, not a fatalistic, passive acceptance of God's pronouncements.

Adam predicates his argument to be patient on "a confident reliance" on God's providence in their lives:

> Then let us seek
> Some safer resolution, which methinks
> I have in view, calling to mind with heed
> Part of our Sentence, that thy Seed shall bruise
> The Serpent's head; piteous amends, unless
> Be meant, whom I conjecture, our grand Foe
> Satan, who in the Serpent hath contriv'd
> Against us in this deceit: to crush his head
> By death brought on ourselves, or childless days
> Resolv'd, as thou proposest; so our Foe
> Shall 'scape his punishment ordain'd, and wee
> Instead shall double ours upon our head.
>
> X, ll. 1028-40

Adam remembers that God had promised to defeat Satan in Eve's "Seed" that "shall bruise / The Serpent's head." If by the "serpent" God meant Satan, Adam conjectures, then His plan is, indeed, superior to Eve's proposal of suicide. Adam and Eve realize that this plan is not only for the good of all mankind but also for their personal benefit. Adam understands that, if he and Eve commit suicide, Satan will not be crushed and, what is more personally significant, they will receive "double" punishment. Adam is concerned with his own personal welfare, and that of Eve, in addition to his concern for the eschatological fulfillment of God's promise.

Milton's theological definition of patience includes awareness of God's goodness, as well as His faithfulness. Adam predicates his advice to Eve in part on God's goodness when he says, "How much more, if we pray him, will his ear / Be open, and his heart of pity incline." He has seen

God's goodness in His bountiful creation; now he rests in the hope that God will be consistent in His character and show goodness toward him even though he has fallen into sin. The goodness which Adam hopes for in relation to his sin, of course, is God's "pity"; he wishes that God might not exact payment from him, but show mercy and fulfill His promise to judge Satan, not Adam (cf. III, ll. 130-32).

Based on his confidence in God's providence and goodness, Adam counsels Eve to patience. The core of his argument follows:

> No more be mention'd then of violence
> Against ourselves, and wilfull barrenness,
> That cuts us off from hope, and savors only
> Rancor and pride, impatience and despite,
> Reluctance against God and his just yoke,
> Laid on our Necks. Remember with what mild
> And gracious temper he both heard and judg'd
> Without wrath or reviling.
>
> X, ll. 1041-47

Adam wishes to "bear [their] inevitable evils with equanimity" and not do "violence against" themselves because impatience would fly in the face of God's goodness toward them. He wishes not to be cut off from hope in the "mild and gracious temper" of God who will, he expects, show mercy to them if they but ask for it (as they do at the end of the book). As well as arguing that they should have patient devotion toward God even in their sin, Adam lists some of their specific sins which cut them off from God. "Rancor," or anger, for example, is the opposite of the fear of God, or the "reverence" of Him and the "dread [of] offending Him above all things" (CE, XVII, p. 61). Anger against God betrays impatience with His providential disposition of the affairs of this life. Pride is, of course, the opposite of humility -- which is the attitude that Adam and Eve take immediately following this speech in their supplication to God for forgiveness (X, ll. 1088-96). Reluctance, the opposite of obedience, would paralyze Adam's wish that he and Eve beg God for mercy. In the speech which precedes their initial penitence, then, Adam seems to understand his position well. He focuses everything that he says to Eve on the character of God and its manifestation in His bounty to them before the fall. In Milton's narrative, Adam and Eve's penitence at the end of Book Ten prompts the realization of God's grace in Books Eleven and Twelve of Paradise Lost -- and, indeed, on into Christ's victories in Paradise Regained. God shows grace to Adam in Michael's visit to encourage him that all is not lost.

It is during Michael's visit that Adam's postlapsarian devotional experience is richest. Michael's message, as well as the kind attitude with which he is instructed by God to deliver it, teaches Adam that he is right to have asked God for forgiveness and to have placed God above Eve's suicidal tendencies. God instructs Michael to "drive out the sinful Pair" (XI, l. 105), but to do so with kindness:

> Yet lest they faint
> At the sad Sentence rigorously urg'd,
> For I behold them soft'ned and with tears
> Bewailing thir excess, all terror hide.
> If patiently thy bidding they obey,
> Dismiss them not disconsolate; reveal
> To Adam what shall come in future days,
> As I shall thee enlighten, intermix
> My Cov'nant in the woman's seed renew'd;
> So send them forth, though sorrowing,
> yet in peace.
>
> XI, ll. 108-17

God intends Michael's chronicle of "history" to Adam to be in part consolatory. He wishes to encourage him, not discourage him; this He does by having Michael promise Adam and Eve their redemption through the woman's seed. The lessons that Adam learns from Michael involve the love of God and obedience to Him. Because of the gratitude and love which Adam bears toward God for His grace, he responds with obedience to His will. His immediate obedience is to leave Eden forever; his motive for obedience is God's grace. Adam says to Michael after he has finished his chronicle of human history:

> Henceforth I learn, that to obey is best,
> And love with fear the only God, to walk
> As in his presence, ever to observe
> His providence, and on him sole depend,
> Merciful over all his works, with good
> Still overcoming evil.
>
> XII, ll. 561-66

This is the thematic climax of the poem in Adam's life. He has fallen, but God has lifted him up in grace. How else can Adam respond except in implicit obedience to God's will, making it "the paramount rule of [his] conduct" (CE, XVII, p. 69)? God's providence is good; therefore, Adam acquiesces. In addition to his obedience, Adam trusts God implicitly. Because of God's mercy, he can "depend" on Him "solely." In The Christian Doctrine, Milton defines Adam's confidence: this is trust, or "wholly repos[ing] on him [God]" (CE, XVII, p. 53). Michael's account of human history, therefore, prompts Adam's immediate trust and obedience.

Trust and obedience are not all that Adam learns from Michael. He goes on to express the patience and meekness which he has learned:

> and by small
> Accomplishing great things, by things deem'd weak
> Subverting worldly strong, and worldly wise
> By simply meek; that suffering for Truth's sake
> Is fortitude to highest victory,
> And to the faithful Death the Gate of Life.
>
> XII, ll. 565b-71

He has learned to allow God's "providence, power, goodness" to gain victory over Satan for him; he has learned to be meek in order to overcome the "worldly strong" and "world wise." In all, Adam has learned "to walk / As in his [God's] presence" at all times in intimate communion with Him because

> Hee to his own a Comforter will send
> The promise of the Father, who shall dwell
> His Spirit within them, and the Law of Faith
> Working through love upon thir hearts shall write,
> To guide them in all truth.
>
> XII, ll. 486-90

Adam is served by Christ as his redeemer, and by the Holy Spirit as his "comforter" and constant guide. Therefore, he is in perpetual devotion to God; his postlapsarian life, because of divine grace, is theocentric.

Michael summarizes Adam's new-found devotional experience at the end of Paradise Lost, when he states:

> only add
> Deeds to thy knowledge answerable, add Faith,
> Add Virtue, Patience, Temperance, add Love,
> By name to come call'd Charity, the soul
> Of all the rest; then will thou not be loath
> To leave this Paradise, but shalt possess
> A paradise within thee, happier far.
>
> XII, ll. 581b-87

Adam is "answerable" for the vastly-increased knowledge about God which Michael's information has given him. He has come to understand God's goodness in the events of history; now he must "add [good] deeds" with an attitude of love toward God. It is love, the "soul of all the rest" of the devout affections, that places God "above all other objects of affection" (CE, XVII, pp. 51 and 53). Before the fall, Adam had gratitude toward God for His beneficence toward him, but that was an external knowledge of God; God was mediated through His blessings. After the fall, on the other hand, Adam comes to love God. This is an internal experience, an active movement toward God on Adam's part. God is mediated now by the "Comforter" and the Son, God's personal agents of redemption.

With the Holy Spirit "who shall dwell . . . within [him] (XII, l. 488), the regenerate Adam takes "paradise" with him -- paradise within him. This is the felix culpa of the experience of devotion in the poem for Adam and Eve. Louis Martz speaks of this paradise within Adam as "the restored Image of God in man" in The Paradise Within (p. 200). With the Comforter dwelling within him, Adam is in a constant devotional relationship with God, walking "as in his presence" throughout his life. Martz insists, as I have throughout this chapter, that this image of God restored (what I have called the devotional experience) is active, not passive. He writes, "The image of God is manifested not in the mere passive possession of certain qualities but in the action, the power to use reason for its proper ends" (p. xiv). It is God's grace and Adam's personal experience of it -- not reason alone, pace Martz -- that accounts for devotion in the poem. Adam's concluding attitude toward God in Paradise Lost is an active, victorious, devotional love of Him above everything else.

Notes
Chapter Three

[1]Hughes, p. xiii; and Hill, p. 119, note 5.

[2]John Holloway, " 'Paradise Lost' and the Quest for Reality," Forum for Modern Language Studies, III (1967), p. 12.

[3]cf. CE, XIV, p. 191.

[4]I accept Hill's interpretation of the nature of Adam's and Eve's need to choose consciously in favor of God even in their prelapsarian state, not Martz's position in The Paradise Within, p. 132, that their love for God before the fall in Paradise Lost was "intuitive" and, therefore, not active.

[5]J.M. Evans, "Paradise Lost" and the Genesis Tradition (New York: Oxford University Press, 1968), p. 269.

[6]Joseph H. Summers, The Muse's Method (Cambridge: Harvard University Press, 1962). p. 71.

[7]cf. Ephesians 5:2. "And walk in love, as Christ also hath loved us, and hath given himself for us an offering and a sacrifice to God for a sweetsmelling savor."

CHAPTER FOUR
Paradise Regained

Paradise Regained presents many problems, at least two of which are relative to the subject of devotion in the poem. The first problem is a theological one, the question of exactly how the Son of God "regains" paradise by foiling Satan's temptations. In Paradise Lost, Adam and Eve are regenerated and given a "Comforter" who provides them with a "paradise within . . . happier far" (XII, l. 1588) than the external paradise of Eden:

> Hee [God] to his own a Comforter will send,
> The promise of the Father, who shall dwell
> His Spirit within them, and the Law of Faith,
> Working through love, upon thir hearts shall
>   write,
> To guide them in all truth, and also arm
> With spiritual Armor, able to resist
> Satan's assaults, and quench his fiery darts.
> XII, ll. 486-92

From these lines, it appears that paradise has already been promised fallen man in his regeneration through God's grace. This paradise is an inner one which Louis Martz identifies in The Paradise Within as "the inward Light by which man is enabled to see a Paradise that lies within the center of the poem [Paradise Lost] and within the center of the mind and memory" (p. 115). How, then, does the Son in Paradise Regained, who is the "True Image of the Father" (IV, l. 596), regain "lost Paradise" and provide a "fairer Paradise" for Adam and Eve (IV, ll. 608 and 613)? It seems that, theologically at least, the Son's appointed task of redemption is unnecessary in that the Father has already promised Adam and Eve a greater paradise in <u>Paradise Lost</u>.

The resolution to this theological problem is simple for Milton. In <u>Paradise Lost</u>, Michael merely reports the information that God the Father has given him about His future plan of redemption through the Son's crucifixion and resurrection. At the end of <u>Paradise Lost</u>, redemption is actually still eschatology. The poem presents prevenient grace, not actual saving grace in operation: Christ has not yet been born nor crucified by the end of <u>Paradise Lost</u>. The "paradise within" of which Adam learns from Michael in the poem, therefore, is yet future for him. In <u>Paradise Regained</u>, however, Milton begins to show God's plan for man's redemption in the Son's victories over Satan's temptations. The Son earns the right to redeem man in his victories in <u>Paradise Regained</u>. He does not, however, complete the task; that would require Calvary.

The second problem in <u>Paradise Regained</u> relates to the protagonist's character development. How can a poem which has the Son of God as its protagonist allow for an experience of devotion? Devotion, especially after its expression by the fallen Adam and Eve in <u>Paradise Lost</u>, involves a growth on man's part toward God that seems impossible for the incarnate Son of God who would surely be in perfect and eternal communication with the Father. In <u>Paradise Lost</u>, Adam and Eve develop a devotion for the Father as their redeemer that they did not possess when they were sinless. Because Adam's sin separates him from God, he must learn to love God by actively obeying Him and, paradoxically, by submitting his will to the Father's. In <u>Paradise Regained</u>, however, the Son is sinless (though not incapable of being tempted by sin);[1] how then can he learn to love God, or even obey Him? Does Milton allow for the Son's character to develop in the poem?

The answer to this question is more complex than the resolution of the other, theological problem. Milton not only allows for the Son to have a valid devotional experience in <u>Paradise Regained</u>, he also develops the character of the Son through his devotional experience. In the course of the narrative, the Son matures in his understanding of his earthly role as man's savior. He develops in his character as the Son of Man to the point at which he is ready to become man's savior at the conclusion of the poem. The angels sing his praise on this theme in their final doxology:

> For though that seat of earthly bliss be fail'd,
> A fairer Paradise is founded now
> For Adam and his chosen Sons, whom thou
> A Savior art come down to reinstall.
>
> IV, ll. 612-15

The significant point about the Son's devotion to the Father in the poem is that he earns his right to become the savior by demonstrating patience with Satan and active obedience to the Father. In order for this development to occur, Milton emphasizes the Son's humanity, while he subordinates his divinity, especially in the temptations which precede the final one at the tower. Because he concentrates more on the Son's humanity than on his divinity, Milton can mature his protagonist in his experience of devotion to the Father.

The opening lines of the poem present Milton's emphasis on the Son's humanity and indicate that the Son will develop in the course of events in the poem:

> I who erewhile the happy Garden sung,
> By one man's disobedience lost, now sing
> Recover'd Paradise to all mankind,
> By one man's firm obedience full tried
> Through all temptation, and the Tempter foil'd
> In all his wiles, defeated and repuls't,
> And Eden rais'd in the waste Wilderness.

> Thou Spirit who led'st this glorious Eremite
> Into the Desert, his victorious Field
> Against the Spiritual Foe, and brought'st him thence
> By proof th'undoubted Son of God, inspire,
> As thou are wont, my prompted Son, else mute,
> And bear through height or depth of nature's bounds
> With prosperous wing full summ'd to tell of deeds
> Above Heroic, though in secret done,
> And unrecorded left through many an Age,
> Worthy t'have not remain'd so long unsung.
>   I, ll. 1-17

In the first verse paragraph, the Son is the "one man" whose "firm obedience" will win redemption for fallen man; he will raise Eden in "the waste Wilderness" of this fallen world. This is the keynote for the poem: as a man, the Son learns to obey the Father and thereby defeat man's "Spiritual Foe," Satan.

In the next paragraph, the poet indicates that, by virtue of the experience of the temptations in the desert, the protagonist will emerge "by proof th'undoubted Son of God." As a result of his victory in the wilderness against Satan, the Son apparently proves himself worthy to be the Savior. The Father makes it clear in His first speech of the poem that the Son earns the right to become the Savior. He speaks of the Son as "This perfect Man, by merit call'd my Son / [Who will] earn Salvation for the Sons of men" (I, ll. 166-67). By virtue of his merit, not because of his divine nature, the Son is worthy to redeem man. Paradise Regained, therefore, is Milton's account of the exercising of the Son's virtue, under Satanic deceit and even attack, to earn salvation for fallen men. In order to demonstrate the process by which the Son earns his rights as Savior, the poet emphasizes his humanity.

Much as a man might engage in an internal debate when he faces uncertainty, the Son goes into the wilderness lost in deep meditation regarding his "Godlike Office." He is unaware of his hunger and thirst for forty days as he considers how best to begin his public work. The poet describes the Son's frame of mind when he enters the wilderness as meditative:

> One day [the Son] forth walk'd alone, the Spirit leading,
> And his deep thoughts, the better to converse
> With solitude, till far from track of men,
> Thought following thought, and step by step led on,
> He enter'd now the bordering Desert wild,
> And with dark shades and rocks environ'd round,
> His holy Meditations thus pursu'd.
>
> I, II. 189-95

The Spirit leads the Son into the "bordering Desert wild." However, the Son is oblivious to his surroundings, lost in "deep thought" and "holy Meditations" regarding his earthly ministry. In Book Two, the poet describes the Son's lonely contemplations in a similar manner:

> [The Son] with holiest Meditations fed,
> Into himself descended, and at once
> All his great work to come before him set;
> How to begin, how to accomplish best
> His end of being on Earth, and mission high.
>
> II. II. 110-14

The purpose for his being in the wilderness is to determine a plan of action for "his great work" of redemption. He has lived thirty years in obscurity and, sensing his need to proclaim his purpose publicly, he seeks to devise a means of accomplishing man's redemption. The Son's character development in Paradise Regained involves his growth in understanding his earthly "mission high."

So significant is the presentation of the protagonist's humanity that virtually no reader of Paradise Regained denies the poet's emphasis on it. Don Cameron Allen attributes the energy and success of the poem to "the fluctuation in this man's [the Son's] knowledge of himself and of his mission"; he states further that this fluctuation "is what makes Paradise Regained more taut in action than Johnson perceived" (p. 118). There is an action in the poem for Allen, the action within the protagonist's character. Barbara Lewalski speaks of the action of the poem in her complex analysis, "Theme and Action in Paradise Regained," as the protagonist's "self-realization" (p. 322). By this term, Lewalski means that the Son actualizes his knowledge about himself (a subject to which I will return shortly) by virtue of his obedience to the Father. In John Milton: Poet, Priest and Prophet, John Spencer Hill understands the focus of Paradise Regained to be the protagonist's "voyage of self discovery . . . and deepening self-awareness" (p. 178). In The Paradise Within, Louis Martz fully agrees with these other statements; in fact, Martz uses the same terminology as Hill does, calling the action of Paradise Regained the "self-discovery of the hero" (p. 180). The point is twofold. The scholarship is virtually unanimous that Milton concentrates on the Son's humanity in Paradise Regained rather than on his divinity.[2] Second, because the Son is human, the critics contend, his character develops in the poem; such references as "self-realization" and "self-discovery" suggest growth and change, not divine stasis.

The question of the final nature of the Son, be it divine or human -- or a hypostatic union of the two -- is a vexed one in the light of The Christian Doctrine. There, Milton subordinates the Son to the Father, denying that he is divine in the same manner as the Father is:

> and so he [the Son] explains himself in the same chapter, after the Jews had misunderstood his saying, [John] x. 38. "believe the works; that ye may know and believe that the Father is in me, and I in him." xiv. 10. "believest thou not that I am in the Father, and the Father in me? the words that I

speak unto you, I speak not of myself, but the Father that dwelleth in me, he doeth the works." Here he [the Son] evidently distinguishes the Father from himself in his whole capacity, but asserts at the same time that the Father remains in him; which does not denote unity of essence, but only intimacy of communion. Secondly, he declares himself to be one with the Father in the same manner as we are one with him; that is, not in essence, but in love, communion, in spirit, in glory.

CE, XIV, pp. 211 and 213

The question is, does Milton depict the protagonist in Paradise Regained in this anti-Trinitarian manner? Don Cameron Allen says not. He does find, however, a pattern to Milton's characterization of the Son as sometimes divine, sometimes human. He writes in The Harmonious Vision, "When Christ is alone, he is human; when he is comforted by Satan, he assumes divinity or, at least, is raised above humanity" (p. 119). The suggestion is helpful but does not give an entirely accurate account of what Milton does with the Son in Paradise Regained. If the Son were divine in his debates with Satan, then the poem would fall flat; there would be no dramatic tension, for the contest would have a fore-ordained result. There is a valid tension in the poem, but it comes from the development of the Son's character as he progresses through patience to obedience to the Father under Satan's pressure.

So important is the Son's humanity to the realization of redemption in Paradise Regained that Mary Ann Radzinowicz insists in Toward "Samson Agonistes": the Growth of Milton's Mind that "the Son's humanity . . . has regained lost paradise" (p. 334). It is because the Son -- as a man -- proves himself worthy of redeeming men that he is victorious in the poem. It is because he defeats Satan, not by virtue of his divine nature (for that would make an unjust combat), but in his humanity that the Son can "earn Salvation for the sons of men" (I, l. 167). It is men who need salvation; it is a man -- "th'exalted man" (I, l. 36) -- who wins it for them.

The regaining of paradise, therefore, is predicated on "one man's firm obedience" (I, l. 4), and that man the second Adam.

Paradoxically, as the Son in Paradise Regained increases in his knowledge of himself and his method of redeeming men, he experiences devotion for the Father. Just as Adam comes to know himself only by submitting obediently to God and receiving His grace, so too the Son in Paradise Regained experiences devotion for the Father only by coming to understand himself fully. This self-knowledge on the Son's part involves both his nature and his mission. Mary Ann Radzinowicz gives us an admirably-brief statement of this paradox in Toward "Samson Agonistes":

> The role of the Son is to achieve self-knowledge in relation to a conception of God, and to act in conformity to that knowledge.
>
> p. 246

Only by understanding his relationship with the Father can the Son realize self-knowledge. That is, the Son comes to understand his own nature only in relation to the Father. Moreover, he must "act in conformity to that knowledge." This action is his mission -- to redeem fallen men. The protagonist comes to realize in the poem, therefore, that he is by nature and, as Hill suggests, by vocation man's Savior (p. 193).

The Son's realization is that, with self-knowledge, which is achieved only by submitting oneself to God, comes proper devotion. This lesson is particularly appropriate in Paradise Regained. Adam learns the same lesson: his postlapsarian devotion demands this type of paradoxical self-knowledge; his prelapsarian devotion is incomplete because he did not put this principle into action. The Son in Paradise Regained, however, provides a paradigm for this type of devotion. In describing Protestant devotion in Protestant Poetics and the Seventeenth Century Religious Lyric, Barbara Lewalski explains how meditations such as the Son's in Paradise Regained can epitomize this type of devotional experience:

> ... Protestant meditation did engage the mind in an effort to penetrate deeply into motives and motions of the psyche, and also to understand the self as the very embodiment of the subject meditated upon. The Word was still to be made flesh, though now in the self of the meditator. . . . . This emphasis contributed to the creation with a new depth and sophistication of psychological insight.
>
> p. 150

Milton has a unique "meditator" in the Son: he is the "Word made flesh"; therefore, he naturally embodies the "subject meditated upon" in himself. This is not to say that it is the Son's divinity that allows the devotional experience in Paradise Regained. As I have already stated, the Son develops into a full understanding of himself as Savior. This process of the Son's increasing awareness of his nature and mission as Savior, gained in the face of Satan's temptations, is exactly how the "Word" becomes "flesh" in the poem. By learning his full humanity, the protagonist becomes a prototype of devotion. But he comes to this experience only through the experiences of the poem and by careful introspection throughout the narrative.

The Son begins this process of "self-realization" and devotion in his opening soliloquy, a passage of a hundred lines in length in which he reflects upon his childhood development. It is spiritual autobiography that demonstrates the Son's understanding of proper devotion: devotion involves the Son's deliberate choice of the Father's will over his own; paradoxically, however, this choice results in the Son's growth in self-knowledge. Self-abnegation is actually the beginning of self-realization. As he enters the "desert wild," the Son is confused: "O what a multitude of thoughts," he says, "at once / Awak'n'd in me swarm" (I, ll. 196-97). In an attempt to bring perspective to his future mission, the Son meditates upon his past, commenting first that he loves the Scriptures, or "the Law of God" as he calls them here, and made their reading his "whole delight" (I, ll. 207-

08). From the very early lines of the Son's first speech, we are aware, therefore, that he knew he was called to a mission: he was "born to promote all truth" (I. I. 206). We know also that he would find that mission revealed in the Scriptures. He remains true to these convictions throughout the poem.

The pressing problem for the Son at the beginning of the poem is not what his task itself is, but rather how to achieve it. It is with this question in mind that he seeks solitude and "wanders" into the desert. As he meditates in this first speech, he remembers that he used to think of accomplishing his mission by military means. He reflects:

> victorious deeds
> Flam'd in my heart, heroic acts; one while
> To rescue Israel from Roman yoke,
> Then to subdue and quell o'er all the earth
> Brute violence and proud Tyrannic pow'r,
> Till truth were freed, and equity restor'd.
>
> I, ll. 215-20

Still searching for his Father's plan, not his own, to redeem man, the Son here considers establishing a political kingdom in which "truth" and "equity" would overrule violence and tyranny. While this is not the Father's mode of redemption, the poet here establishes the Son's inclination toward active involvement to make a plan work. However, the Son comes to understand that the Father does not intend for him to establish a political kingdom yet, and so he rejects his military aspirations as inappropriate to his task. The Son does come to realize by his consideration of military strength, however, one important phase of his mission, and that is "to rescue Israel from Roman yoke" (I, I. 217). He is learning here to submit to the Father's will in all points of his mission -- method as well as purpose.

Having rejected martial force as an appropriate means to complete his task, the Son turns to persuasion as the possible mode of freeing Israel. He says that he

> Yet held it more humane, more heavenly, first
> By winning words to conquer willing hearts,
> And make persuasion do the work of fear.
>
> I, ll. 22-23

Significantly, the Son attempts to find a method of completing his purpose which is both human and divine. The decision not to coerce men by martial force to submit to the Father's redemption, but rather to win men's wills to salvation indicates the Son's enlarged perspective of his task. He understands early in the poem that men must wish redemption of their own free wills.

After considering political and rhetorical methods of achieving redemption, the Son returns to the Scriptures, or "the law and Prophets," and ponders again how to obey God's mandate to him. His examination of the Old Testament turns his attention toward the Jewish Messiah. He "soon found of whom they spake": it was himself. What is more, he tells us:

> This chiefly, that my way must lie
> Through many a hard assay even to the death,
> Ere I the promised Kingdom can attain,
> Or work Redemption for mankind, whose sins'
> Fell weight must be transferr'd upon my head.
>
> II, ll. 263-67

He comes to understand that he must suffer "through many a hard assay even to the death" if he is to "work Redemption for mankind."

No doubt the scriptural reference that the Son has in mind as prophesying his suffering is in Isaiah:

> But he was wounded for our transgressions, he was bruised for our iniquities; the chastisement of our peace was upon him; and with his stripes we are healed.
> All we like sheep have gone astray; we have turned every one to his own way; and the Lord hath laid on him the iniquity of us all.
>
> Isaiah 53: 5-6

The Son's allusion to the Book of Isaiah here makes it clear that he knows before he meets Satan that his task is to be a painful one; yet he does not waiver.

The Son's response to the prophesied suffering is the climax of his first speech. "Yet neither thus dishearten'd or dismay'd," he declares, "The time prefixt I waited" (I, ll. 268-69). Unlike Eve in Paradise Lost who misconstrues her situation and chooses unwisely to act outside of God's commands, the Son here chooses to subordinate his will to the Father's and await His timing to begin his Messianic responsibilities. The Son's decision to obey the Father demonstrates the central paradox of his devotion throughout the poem: by what appears at first to be passive submission, the Son begins to earn the right to "work Redemption for mankind" (I, l. 266). John Spencer Hill explains the paradox in John Milton: Poet, Priest and Prophet this way:

> [The Son learns] to will to relax the will, a spiritual state which is the apex of self-knowledge and the apotheosis of human potential.
>
> pp. 182-83

The proper way to self-knowledge for the Son is to obey the Father. The Son's path toward self-knowledge lies through pain. To be man's savior, he must suffer; it is this suffering that he begins to confront in Paradise Regained. As Hill states, the Son "must assist divine disposal [the soteriological mission] by his own responsive choices" (p. 179). The Son's response to the Father is to choose suffering. This choice leads him both to knowledge of himself and devotion to the Father.

Immediately following this decision to obey the Father even in suffering, the Son goes to the river Jordan and, at his baptism, hears the Father's public pronouncement of approval upon his obedience. He then obeys the promptings "by some strong motion" to enter the wilderness and there await further understanding from the Father:

> And now by some strong motion I am led
> Into this Wilderness, to what intent
> I learn not yet; perhaps I need not know;
> For what concerns my knowledge God reveals.
>
> I, II. 290-93

So the stage is set for the temptations that will test the Son's "merit" to redeem mankind.

The testing of the Son's worthiness to be man's savior involves the Son's patience in the face of Satan's temptations in addition to his obedience to the Father. Satan tests the Son's patience in that he tempts the Son to wrest power to himself prematurely, before the Father's "time prefixt" (I, l. 269). The Son's patience, which is a passive virtue, involving the Son's ability to withstand Satan, and his obedience, which is active in that it deliberately places the Father's will above the Son's, are important expressions of love for the Father. Barbara Lewalski summarizes these two experiences in her commentary on the temptation at the tower in "Theme and Action in Paradise Regained." She writes that the Son's "journey to self-understanding . . . images forth the passive endurance he will display at the Crucifixion [and] . . . turn[s] this passion [the crucifixion] into a dramatic act of conquest over Satan" (p. 344). Just as the crucifixion is paradoxical in that it involves both suffering and victory for the Savior, so too the temptations are paradoxical in that they involve the Son's patience with Satan and his obedience to the Father; they are two expressions of the same devotional motive on the Son's part for his whole earthly mission -- his willing love for the Father.

The narrative of the actual temptations is much lengthier and more complex in Milton's account of it than in any of the gospel versions. Accordingly, scholars have divided and arranged the temptations in various ways -- usually in categories which assist their central arguments. In John Milton: Poet, Priest and Prophet, for instance, John Spencer Hill copies Milton's division of Paradise Regained into its four books, each one furthering, in Hill's account, the Son's sense of "vocation" (pp. 175-94). In The Milton Handbook, James Holly Hanford divides the temptations as follows. The first temptation is Satan's crude appeal to the Son's hunger in Book One. The second temptation is that of the "Kingdoms of the World," which includes the profuse banquet at the beginning of Book Two; the discussion of "glory"; Parthia; Rome; and, finally, Greece.   The third temptation, according to Hanford, is that at the tower in Book Four (pp. 274-79).   However, neither Hanford's nor Hill's approach reveals to advantage the development of the Son's experience of devotion in the course of the temptations. Let me, therefore, following Hanford's hint that the gospel account closest to Milton's narrative is Luke's (p. 271), return to the fourth chapter of the Gospel of Luke. Luke recounts the story this way: Satan tempts the Son first with food (verse 3); next he tempts with "all the kingdoms of the world" (verses 5-7); and, finally, he tempts Christ at the "pinnacle" of the temple (verses 9-13). Accordingly, the temptations in Paradise Regained would be structured in the following pattern. The first temptation includes the two temptations of the Son's hunger, the crude appeal in Book One and the luxurious banquet in Book Two. The second temptation is comprised of the "kingdoms of the world," including Parthia, Rome and Greece; Satan tempts the Son here with "glory" and "learning," as well. The third temptation is Satan's attempt to have the Son cast himself down from the tower in Book Four. This sequence reveals the development of the Son's patience into obedience.

The first temptation, that one which appeals to the Son's bodily hunger after he has passed "four times ten days" (II, l. 245) in the wilderness without food, tests the Son's patience in three ways. The most obvious test of the Son's patience is of his physical endurance: will he, after protracted hunger, change stones into bread to satisfy his own needs? Even this simple temptation is a test of the Son's earlier statement that "what concerns my knowledge God reveals" (I, l. 293); the temptation questions whether or not the Son can trust the Father to provide for his physical needs as a man in time. The Son replies "sternly" (I, l. 407) to Satan's temptation and offers Job as an example of godly patience in the face of physical adversity (I, ll. 424-46). Clearly, the Son perceives this first temptation as a test of his patient trust in the Father's providence; he responds with a "confident reliance" in God's provision for him (cf. CE, XVII, p.67).

The second test of the Son's patience in the first temptation comes with the "Table richly spread in regal mode" (II, l. 340). This is a test of the Son's temperance. The question here is not so much the need of food for survival; rather, it is the degree of control which the Son has over his senses. Appropriately, Jesus replies, "temperately" to this temptation, condemning Satan's "pompous delicacies" as "specious gifts" (II, ll. 378; 390-91). The Son responds to the temptation to indulge himself hedonistically with appropriate self-control.

Satan's final test in the first temptation is a subtle attack on the Son's patient trust in the Father. This is the temptation to wealth -- wealth that Satan appeals to as a means to supply a myriad of other wants to which Satan returns in his second temptation, that of the worldly kingdoms. The Son replies "patiently" (II, l. 433), debating logically with Satan the uses of wealth in principle. In his final dismissal of Satan's testing of his physical desires, the Son states:

> . . . [to] worship God aright,
> Is yet more Kingly; this attracts the Soul,
> Governs the inner man, the nobler part.
>
> II, ll. 475-77

This is a devotional expression of temperance, one which predicates self-control on the "worship [of] God." Therefore, the Son rests his refusal of Satan's first temptation (to allow him to supply the Son's bodily wants) on his worship, or love, of the Father. The fact that the Son moves from reacting "sternly" in his initial answer to Satan to replying "patiently" at the end of the first temptation demonstrates the care with which the poet develops the Son's patience in this temptation. This temptation is the first test of the Son's "endurance"; at this point it is his bodily endurance after forty days of starvation that is under attack.

Satan's second temptation of the Son is the complex series of tests which the kingdoms of the world present. Satan taunts the Savior with examples of young emperors, such as Alexander the Great and Julius Caesar, who rose to power earlier in their lives than the Son appears to be rising; "Thy years are ripe, and over-ripe," he challenges the Son (III, l. 31). The Son's reply is a quiet, but effective, repudiation of the temptation to premature political glory and the wealth on which such fame is predicated. The Son demonstrates his patience as he replies "calmly" with this statement:

> Thou neither dost persuade me to seek wealth
> For Empire's sake, nor Empire to affect
> For glory's sake by all thy argument.
>
> III, ll. 44-47

The statement demonstrates the Son's perception of Satan's lies about wealth, power and fame: recalling the earlier temptation to wealth, the Son repudiates money as the proper base of power; he rejects the temptation to seize political power at this moment in his life because to do so would be to disobey the Father whose time is "not yet ripe"; he introduces the speech on false and true glory, denying that political power is the proper source of glory. The Son thinks of glory as a result of power that is properly used to glorify God.

The Son's speech on the false "blaze of fame" as opposed to "true glory and renown" (III, ll. 44-64) is an important example of his experience of devotion. The speech is a microcosm of the Son's devotion in the poem, modulating his patience into obedience. The Son first explains the error of Satan's perception of glory:

> For what is glory but the blaze of fame,
> The people's praise, if always praise unmixt?
> And what the people but a herd confus'd?
>
> III, ll. 47-49

The Son find the opinions of the "miscellaneous rabble" (l. 50) unreliable, even undesirable, as a measure of glory. However, he does not conclude his statement with this repudiation; rather, he immediately goes on to define "true glory and renown":

> This is true glory and renown, when God
> Looking on th'Earth, with approbation marks
> The just man, and divulges him through Heaven
> To all his Angels, who with true applause
> Recount his praises.
>
> III, ll. 60-64

True glory is God's "approbation," or approval, not man's. The Son seeks the applause only of the Father and the angels because they praise the "just" man. Political glory, which brings with it the adulation of people, has no attraction for the Son. He has already determined to obey God, not to rest in the praises of men. In his speech on fame, therefore, the Son moves beyond the repudiation of an evil (here the sin of presumptuous political power) to the active commitment to seeking the Father's approbation before that of men.

Repeating Satan's earlier use of examples to affirm his point, the Son next offers two "just" men who won God's praise and who are, therefore, worthy of emulation: Job and Socrates. One is a biblical hero, the other a classical philosopher, but both are obedient heroes in the Son's eyes because they were patient men. The Son's praise of Job's and Socrates' patience is his most direct statement on the subject of godly patience in the poem. In The Christian Doctrine, Milton defines patience as "that whereby we acquiesce in the promises of God, through a confident reliance on his divine providence, power and goodness, and bear inevitable evils with equanimity, as the dispensation of the supreme Father, and sent for our good" (CE, XVII, p. 67). Job and Socrates represent different types of patience in the poem, Socrates an example of "patience within [him]self," and Job an example of "patience toward God," to use Mary Ann Radzinowicz' terms in Toward "Samson Agonistes" (p. 238).

What better example of "patience toward God," or devotional patience, than the biblical Job? The opening scene in the Book of Job is in heaven, with a conversation in progress between the Father and Satan about Job. "Hast thou considered my servant Job," the Father asks Satan, "that there is none like him in the earth?" (Job 1:8) The Father offers Job to Satan as an example of a devout man. Satan's reply, "Doth Job fear God for nought?" (Job 1:9), challenges the Father that Job does not love the Father for Himself, but for the material abundance that God has bestowed upon him. Clearly the writer of the Book of Job wishes his readers to think in cosmological terms, the contest for Job's soul emphatically one between God and Satan. The story is well-known: bereft of all his family except a critical wife; spoiled of all his wealth; afflicted with boils from head to heel; and saddled with self-righteous "friends," Job waits patiently for God. He says,

> Naked came I out of my mother's womb, and naked shall I
> return thither; the Lord gave, and the Lord hath taken away;
> blessed be the name of the Lord.
>
> Job 1:21

Job patiently -- almost passively -- accepts God's sovereign control over all that he possessed, now taken from him.

Job's patience is not limited, however, to passive acceptance of present evil. Patience in the face of present "inevitable evils" is good, but "confident reliance" on God for the future is better. In the nineteenth chapter of the Book of Job, the protagonist says, "I know that my redeemer liveth," and again, "in my flesh I shall see God" (Job 19:25 and 26b). Job's patience extends beyond himself, even beyond faith in God for the needs of the moment; Job's faith is a type of devotional love for God that "confidently" awaits God's vindication of his sufferings. The Son's offer to Satan of Job as an example of "patience toward God" is an implicit condemnation of Satan's impatience to be exalted above God; more importantly, Job is an example of a man who manifests devout patience in his life.

The Son contrasts Job with the example of Socrates, a man whose patience is more passive than active:

> Poor Socrates (who next more memorable?)
> By what he taught and suffer'd for so doing,
> For truth's sake suffering death unjust, lives now
> Equal in fame to proudest Conquerors.
>
> III, ll. 96-99

Socrates was executed for allegedly teaching doctrines that were contrary to the worship of state gods. The Son states that Socrates was executed unjustly for seeking "truth." Socrates is an example of "patience within oneself." He did not have the Hebrew God, the Son's Father, to "inspire" him as Job did. His patience, therefore, is a result of his own character. Socrates' patience is a remarkable instance of patience that comes from the strength of personal convictions -- not patience toward God.

The Son concludes his speech on the patience of Job and Socrates by reminding Satan that he himself is patient because he has "confident reliance on [the Father's] divine providence" in his life. He says,

> Shall I seek glory then, as vain men seek
> Oft not deserv'd? I seek not mine, but his
> Who sent me, and thereby witness whence I am.
>
> III, ll. 150-07

This is an example, not only of patience, but also of the obedience which the Son learns in Paradise Regained. "Obedience is that virtue whereby we propose to ourselves the will of God as the paramount rule of our conduct, and serve him alone," Milton writes in The Christian Doctrine (CE, XVII, p. 69). The Son is an emissary with a responsibility to obey his Father. All of Satan's temptations, in one way or another, tempt him to make his own will and his desires supreme, not the Father's. Therefore, the most significant practical expression of devotion in the poem is the Son's obedience to his Father's will. It is important that, in the words with which the Son finally rejects the temptation to political glory, obedience shows love: his obedience is a "witness" of the motivation for his mission, the Father's offer of grace to fallen men.

Obedience is certainly important for Milton; it is in Adam's case in Paradise Lost as well as in the Son's case in Paradise Regained. But the motive for obedience is more important for Milton. Adam obeys because of the love which God's goodness prompts in him after the fall (cf. PL, XII, ll. 469-84); in Paradise Regained, the Son obeys the Father because of the love he bears Him. Immediately after the Son's statement that he seeks God's glory, not his own, Satan replies that even God "seeks glory"; therefore, if the Son is to be like his Father, Satan suggests, he must seek glory, too. The Savior's reply is quick and incisive; it is "fervent" because the Son perceives the Father's character to be impugned by Satan:

> since his work all things produc'd,
> Though chiefly not for glory as prime end,
> But to show forth his goodness, and impart
> His good communicable to every soul
> Freely; of whom what could he less expect
> Than glory, and benediction, that is thanks?
>
> III, ll. 122-27

The Son makes it clear to Satan that, though God is worthy of all glory for His having created everything that is, His motive in creating was to show His goodness. Therefore, not because God created for glory, but because He created at all, the Savior argues, He deserves praise. This is devout love, or the preference of God "above all other objects of affection" and "the desire to bring Him glory" (CE, XVII, pp. 51 and 53). The Son's love for the Father motivates his desire to glorify Him, not himself. This is important in Milton's view of obedience. The Son is not God's puppet in Paradise Regained; he is an individual with free will who shows his love of the Father by his unforced obedience to His will.

With his accounts of the glories of Parthia and Rome, Satan redoubles his temptations of the Son to disobey the Father's will in his earthly ministry. Ironically, however, the Son learns more about his work of redemption from Satan's attacks. In the early verses of Book Four, the Son demonstrates that he, like Job and Socrates, is a patient hero. His temptation of the Savior to temporal, political glory having failed, Satan tempts with classical eloquence. The Son rejects this temptation on the basis that his kingdom is yet future. He can wait, he says:

> Know therefore when my season come to sit
> On David's Throne, it shall be like a tree

Spreading and overshadowing all the Earth
IV, ll. 146-48

And of my Kingdom there shall be no end:
Means there shall be to this, but what the means,
Is not for thee to know, nor me to tell.
IV, ll. 151-53

The Savior is willing to wait patiently for the time appointed in the Father's will to take his throne. He is unwilling to wrest power to himself too soon and thereby be forced to make use of Satan's power to achieve his goal. Though the Savior's comment suggests that his knowledge of his future kingdom is greater than Satan's, he still demonstrates patience; that is, he has a "confident reliance on [God's] divine providence, power and goodness" and he is, therefore, willing to bear Satan's onslaughts "with equanimity, as the dispensation of the Father, sent for [his] good" (CE, XVII, p. 67). The Son's patience is not fatalism and passivity. It is confidence in God's plan, or His providence, and His ability (or "power") to fulfill that plan in men's lives through his own obedience. In his deliberately submitting his will to the Father's, the Son's patience becomes active obedience.

Satan's most intensive and subtle temptation of the Son is his final volley in the temptation of the kingdoms of the world. He marshals all of his deceit and subtlety to win the Son away from Hebrew wisdom to the best of Gentile wisdom, namely Greek culture. He wishes the Son to grant that Gentile wisdom is as legitimate as the canonical Hebrew wisdom. The heart of this temptation is here:

All knowledge is not couch't in Moses' Law,
The Pentateuch or what the Prophets write;
The Gentiles also know, and write,and teach
To admiration, led by Nature's light.
IV, ll. 225-28

The first implication of this statement is that Hebrew wisdom is incomplete in that it needs Gentile wisdom to augment it. The second implication is that Gentile wisdom is superior to Hebrew because it lacks the supernatural inspiration of the Hebrew writers and yet still communicates truth. Were the Savior to grant this, he would no longer have an adequate base on which to predicate his call to redeem mankind and, therefore, could not be obedient to the call at all. Early in the poem, we must remember, he had determined from the scriptures alone that he was called to redeem men (cf. I, ll. 207-08), and now that foundation is under attack.

Satan's temptation is lengthy and compelling. He moves on quickly from his premise that the Hebrew scriptures are inadequate by themselves to provide truth, to "gloze" it over with appealing examples of the beauties of Gentile literature. Specifically, Satan presents Plato and his Academy as a pristine pastoral retreat. Plato is the "Attic Bird" who "warbles" notes of wisdom all "summer long." Even the "bees' industrious murmur oft invites / To studious musing" (IV, ll. 245-59). Satan perverts the pastoral into a studious, but finally passive, retreat from the Savior's call to redeem mankind. This temptation is to passive meditation without practical good works; such a posture would be disobedience of the Father on the Son's part and an inadequate expression of active devotion for the Father.

Satan further amplifies his temptation with references to Greek music, oratory and philosophy, all intended to dissipate the Son's attention upon obeying God's mandate into an indefinite postponement of the responsibility. Satan tempts the Son with "Aeolian charms and Dorian Lyric Odes," with the works of "the famous Orators" and finally with "sage Philosophy next," Socrates, the Peripatetics, Epicureans and Stoics offered as specific examples (IV, ll. 257-80). The Son listens patiently to the long list of Greek writers.

The Son's patience with Satan is not, however, acquiescence. Very quickly, he focuses his repudiation of Satan's temptation on his initial premise that Gentile literature provides legitimate truths that the Hebrew scriptures lack:

> Alas! What can they teach, and not mislead;
> Ignorant of themselves, of God much more,
> And how the world began, and how man fell
> Degraded by himself, on grace depending?
> Much of the soul they talk, all awry,
> And in themselves seek virtue, and to themselves
> All glory arrogate, to God give none.
>
> IV, ll. 309-15

This is the Son's most categorical rejection of Satan's temptation using Gentile glory and culture. The Son claims that the Gentiles are wrong in that they neither understand God nor give glory to Him for what He has done. He makes it clear that the proper perspective on God is to love Him: He has created all things and, in His grace, He has provided a plan of redemption for fallen men. Therefore, the Son defends his obedience to the Father on the basis of his love for Him; Gentile learning, then, is ultimately inadequate as devotion because it does not finally take God into account as creator or redeemer.

Far from having achieved their aim of destroying the Savior, Satan's temptations have only helped the Son to articulate a defense of his obedience to God. That defense is his love of God above everything else, because of His goodness to men in creation and redemption. It is in this sense that the Son is the "second Adam" in Paradise Regained. Adam and Eve proved their disdain for God in their disobedience in the garden of Eden in Paradise Lost; the Savior shows his love for God in his obedience to Him in Paradise Regained.

The temptation of "all the kingdoms of the world," especially the powerful appeal of Greek learning, is a crisis in the Son's developing devotional experience in Paradise Regained. The Son demonstrates his patience, rooted in his worship of God, in his rejection of Satan's first temptation to satisfy his bodily hunger by reverting to means outside of the Father's provision for him; this temptation manifests the Son's devout patience predicated on the Father's care for the Son.

The second temptation, however, demands more of the Son than his passive refusal; it demands that he put forward some active alternatives to Satan's offerings. Against Satan's temptation of false glory, the Son espouses the "true glory and renown" of God's "approbation" (III, ll. 60-61). Against the natural wisdom of the Gentiles which Satan suggests is necessary for a man to have complete knowledge, the Son champions Hebrew wisdom alone. Truth, he says, rests only in that literature in which

> God is prais'd aright, and Godlike men,
> The Holiest of Holies, and his Saints:
> Such are from God inspir'd, not such from thee [Satan].
>
> IV, ll. 348-51

This second temptation, then, prepares the Son for Satan's final attack by soliciting his active obedience to the Father; consistently aware of always obeying the Father, he clearly declares himself the Messiah in this temptation. William G. Riggs comments on the effects of temptation on the Savior in The Christian Poet in "Paradise Lost":

> In contemplation of his own acts and potential for action, the Miltonic hero [here, the Son] discovers God in himself. Through temptation he is perfected in obedience and rectitude.
>
> p. 188

The Son enters the final temptation, ready to secure his calling as mankind's redeemer by defeating Satan one more time.

The Son does indeed defeat Satan one more time, though the outcome of the conflict is never in doubt, of course, for the reader who knows the New Testament. There is, however, a major difference in the presentation of the Son's defeat of Satan at the tower. No longer does the poet qualify the Son's response to Satan. Earlier in the poem, the poet notes that the Son replies to Satan in a variety of ways: he replies, for instance, "sternly" (I, l. 407); "temperately" (II, l. 378); "patiently" (II, l. 433); "calmly" (III, l. 43); "fervently" (III, l. 121); and "sagely" (IV, l.. 285). Not once in the first two temptations does the Son reply to Satan without the poet's qualification. It is significant that, in the final temptation, the poet introduces the Son's climactic repudiation of Satan with the simple "To whom thus Jesus" (IV, l. 560). The statement which follows is remarkable because of its brevity and its effect on the Tempter:

> Also it is written,
> Tempt not the Lord thy God, he said and stood.
> But Satan smitten with amazement fell.
>
> IV, ll. 560b-62

The Son merely "stood." Apparently by the very power of his character, the Son here vanquishes Satan whose test of the Savior is ultimately tempting God the Father. In his humanity, the Son defeats Satan; by virtue of the patience and obedience which he learned under Satan's attack, the Son overcomes the Tempter.

The Savior's defeat of the Tempter is the climax of Paradise Regained. The brevity of the poet's narration of the event is a remarkable break with his earlier practice; as a result, the event is all the more effective for its intensity. A.S.P. Woodhouse notes that the Son's action at the tower is the "supreme act of obedience and trust."[3] The Son's confident refusal to be trapped by Satan to do anything but stand is the final active assertion of his obedience to the Father to await His time, and his trust in God to defend him at the moment against Satan's attempts to harm him. In John Milton: Poet, Priest and Prophet, Hill writes of the Son's final action at the pinnacle as "manifesting once again that selfless patience and obedience to the Father" (p. 192). Hill, too, regards the Son's strength to be the result of his developing character in the narrative. In fact, Hill thinks of the tower temptation as the one in which the Son reverses combat roles with Satan and takes the offensive against man's "spiritual Foe" (I, l. 10). Hill states, "Action, formerly the essence of temptation, is now, as the Son embarks on his messianic mission, enjoined as a vocational necessity" (p. 193). Seen in this light, the temptations in Paradise Regained try the Son's merit to be man's savior and find it adequate. The Son progresses beyond patience with Satan to obedience to the Father. The action is now the Savior's, not Satan's.

This is why the angels praise the Savior at the end of the poem: he has "recovered paradise [for] all mankind / By [his] firm obedience" to God's command (I, ll. 3-4). They are grateful that, because of what the Savior has done, man will receive grace:

> For though that seat of earthly bliss be fail'd,
> A fairer Paradise is founded now
> For Adam and his chosen Sons, whom thou
> A Savior art come down to reinstall.
>
> IV, ll. 612-15

The Savior does not create a new paradise; he merely "reinstalls" the one that had been lost by Adam's and Eve's disobedience. This restored paradise, however, is a paradise within -- as it is at the end of Paradise Lost. It is, as Louis Martz indicates in The Paradise Within, the "restored image of God in man, the paradise within" (p. 200) that the Son gives to fallen men. In the words of the angels' doxology, it is the

> True Image of the Father, whether thron'd
> In the bosom of bliss, and light of light
> Conceiving, or remote from Heaven, enshrin'd
> In fleshly Tabernacle, and human form,

> Wand'ring the Wilderness, whatever place,
> Habit, or state, or motion, still expressing
> The Son of God
>
> IV, ll. 596-602a

The Savior is able to "earn" man's redemption at the end of Paradise Regained because his obedience to the Father has made it possible to "reinstall" the image of the Father in regenerate men. The Son's devotional experience in Paradise Regained is, as Barbara Lewalski suggests about Protestant devotion in the seventeenth century, a process whereby the "Word" becomes "flesh."

The Son's victory is not his alone; he regains paradise for fallen men. Milton's presentation of the Son's actions in Paradise Regained, therefore, "represent[s] the process of recovery, the recovery of a paradise within" (Riggs, p. 187) for every man. The Son is not only an image of the Father, he is also an image for man of paradise regained. He is, in Riggs' term, an exemplar, "a crucial instance of the labor all men must undertake" (p. 186) if they are to realize the paradise within that the Savior's obedience to the Father makes possible. He is an example of the experience of devotion which the first Adam's fall necessitates and the second Adam's obedience makes possible. The Son's experience of devotion in Paradise Regained is, in Milton's view, an example of the devotion that is possible for all men, not the theological premise on which God's offer of devotion to fallen men is predicated. It is, finally, in his full humanity, not his divinity, that the Son experiences devotion for the Father developing in the poem; it is in the Son's humanity that Milton finally manifests the experience of devotion in Paradise Regained.

Notes
Chapter Four

[1]Barbara Lewalski, "Theme and Action in Paradise Regained, in Milton's Epic Poetry: Essays on "Paradise Lost" and "Paradise Regained", ed. C. A. Patrides (Harmondsworth, England: Penguin Books, 1967), p. 323. All subsequent references to this work will be cited in the text of the book.

[2]cf. Hanford, p. 274. Compare also the following:

Douglas Bush, John Milton: A Sketch of His Life and Writings (New York: Collier Books, 1964), p. 185.

Denis Saurat, Milton: Man and Thinker (New York: The Dial Press, Inc., 1925), p. 278.

[3]A.S.P. Woodhouse, "Theme and Pattern in Paradise Regained," University of Toronto Quarterly, XXV (1956-57), p. 181.

CHAPTER FIVE
Samson Agonistes

In the capture and apparent defeat of the biblical hero, Samson, Milton gives his clearest expression of the experience of devotion. The choice of Samson as the protagonist of his final poem frees Milton from the encumbrances that attached to the devotional experience in both Paradise Lost and Paradise Regained. In Paradise Lost, Milton faced the difficulty of providing a valid experience of devotion for his readers in the innocent experiences of Adam and Eve before they fell. It is sin, ironically, that completes Adam and Eve's experience of devotion and demands that their obedience to and love for God be active and voluntary expressions of devotion on their parts. For two-thirds of the poem, therefore, Milton must be careful to insure that Adam and Eve's innocent devotion does not seem inadequate for a fallen reader. In Paradise Regained Milton must maintain a finely-tuned tension between the two natures of his protagonist as God and man if he is to express a mature devotion at all. Because of the problems that an over-emphasis early in the poem on the Son's divinity would present to his experience of devotion, the poet concentrates on developing the humanity of the Son under Satan's temptations so as to demonstrate that the Son is worthy to become man's Savior. With Samson, however, Milton is free of both the untried innocence of Adam and Eve in the first eight books of Paradise Lost and the unexercised sinlessness of the Son as he enters the desert in Paradise Regained. Samson is a fallen man. In regards to the experience of devotion, Samson Agonistes is Milton's Everyman.[1]

Samson Agonistes begins with the protagonist apparently defeated. Both internal and external forces in Samson's life have combined before the beginning of the poem to bring him down in defeat. Once Israel's champion against the Philistines, Samson is now "eyeless in Gaza"; he has been blinded by his captors and imprisoned "at the Mill with slaves" (l. 41). What is worse, he is soon to be called upon to "stain [his] vow of Nazarite" (l. 1386) and become the entertainment at the Philistines' celebration of Dagon's victory over Samson's God, Jehovah. All of this misery is the immediate result of Dalila's betrayal of Samson -- her husband, in Milton's account -- to her people. In Milton's view, however, the cause of Samson's initial fall is not the faithlessness of a "heathen" woman, but the weaknesses of Samson himself.

Samson's weaknesses are his pride, his impatience, his disobedience to God and his fear that he has been cast off by God forever. It is these weaknesses that the the action of the poem forces Samson to confront. Significantly, Samson does not examine himself apart from God; rather, by examining himself in relation to God, he learns the humility and patience which give him the obedience and hope that he needs to serve God once again. The action of the poem is the development in Samson's character of devotion to God. There are no angels, no direct revelations sent from God and no supernatural appearances by Satan in the poem to share the reader's attention with Samson. There are not even any lengthy claims to divine inspiration by Samson that might direct the reader's attention away from the simple, natural development of the protagonist's character; only once in the poem does Samson lay claim to any "inspiration" which affects his action, and that is to "some rousing motions" which "dispose" his thoughts to "something extraordinary" (ll. 1382-83). In Toward "Samson Agonistes: the Growth of Milton's Mind, Mary Ann Radzinowicz notes that there is not even a poet-speaker, apart from the fallible chorus, to comment on the action of the poem (p. 185). Milton gives us Samson alone with his visitors, "struggling," as Galbraith M. Crump says in his "Introduction" to Twentieth-Century Interpretations of "Samson Agonistes", to "define himself within the vast dimensions of a theocentric universe."[2] This is the focus of the poem: Samson and his God.

The action of the poem, then, is the development of Samson's character specifically from pride to humility, from impatience to patience, from disobedience to obedience, and from despair to hope which results from his devotion to God. John Spencer Hill perceives the action of Samson Agonistes to be the protagonist's "progressively more acute spiritual awareness" (p. 151); Hill's comment implies that Samson matures spiritually in a teleological manner, one lesson predicated on the previous one. Balachandra Rajan disagrees with Hill on this point. In The Lofty Rhyme, Rajan states that Samson's growth is not a progressive movement toward "self-knowledge," but rather a "movement into dejection and out of it."[3] While there is a "restoration" (p. 144) of Samson's equilibrium for Rajan, it results from dejection.[4] I think that Mary Ann Radzinowicz understands Samson's character development correctly when she states that he matures spiritually in the poem, though not always progressively. This, she states, is normal for a fallen man. As proof, Radzinowicz quotes Samson on Dalila:

> So let her go, God sent her to debase me,
> And aggravate my folly who committed
> To such a viper his most sacred trust
> Of secrecy, my safety, and my life.

II. 999-1002

Commenting on this speech, she observes that "Samson's regeneration does not trace a simple curve; like all suffering men, he can and does lapse from new levels of insight back into old positions. Such regressions testify to the painful nature of change and permit change at a pace tolerable to the human psyche" (p. 237). There is development, therefore, though not a simple one, for Samson.

It is important to recognize that Milton develops the character of Samson through action. Were Samson to remain "blind to the spiritual significance of his suffering," as William G. Madsen asserts he does in "From Shadowy Types to Truth" (p. 95), his final act of pulling down the temple on both the Philistines and himself would be insignificant. If Samson does develop, he must do so in response to his suffering. The Chorus sees Samson's act as the inscrutable vindication of God's Providence that "All is best, though we oft doubt / What th'unsearchable dispose / Of highest wisdom brings about" (ll. 1475-77). Manoa, the Israelite who least perceives God's hand in Samson's life, finds "no time for lamentation now" (l. 1078) when he hears of Samson's death. And Samson himself predicts, "This day will be remarkable in my life / By some great act, or of my days the last" (ll. 1388-89). Samson's character develops in relation to God. It is not, as Madsen insists, that Samson does not develop spiritually; it is rather that he is engaged throughout the action of the poem in "an internal struggle toward self-knowledge," or a psychomachia (Crump, p. 6). Samson develops spiritually as a fallen man does -- imperfectly and tentatively. Radzinowicz aptly declares that the meaning of Samson's life is "to grow toward knowledge of God. . . . A more profound faith . . . then emerge[s] in action" (p. 250).

Samson's prime character flaw is his pride. He has done great things for God and Israel, delivering them temporarily from the hands of the Philistines. Even in prison at the beginning of the poem, he displays self-pity which is a manifestation of his pride; he chafes under his incarceration. From the outset of the poem, he struggles with his self-pity on the one hand and his personal responsibility for his own calamity on the other. Even though the feast in honor of Dagon provides him with a rest from his forced labor, he cannot escape his own shame. He laments:

> Ease to the body some, none to the mind
> From restless thoughts, that like a deadly swarm
> Of hornets arm'd no sooner found alone,
> But rush upon me thronging, and present

Times past, what once I was, and what am now.
O wherefore was my birth from Heaven foretold
Twice by an Angel?

ll. 18-24a

These are not the words of a man who accepts responsibility for his actions and repents of his wrongs. Samson shifts responsibility onto God whose angels foretold his great destiny and then betrayed him along the way by allowing him to be ignominiously defeated. Samson regards himself as a victim of his own thoughts, which, like a "deadly swarm of hornets," descend upon him the minute that he is at rest from his physical labor, "found alone." He depicts himself as the receiver of wrongs, not their originator. This is the first picture that the reader has of Samson; with a great deal of self-pity, he laments the lot which has been forced upon him.

In his first speech, Samson demonstrates his injured pride in his lament over the extremity of his fall from national deliverer to slave. In anguish, he cries out:

O glorious strength
Put to the labor of a Beast, debas't
Lower than bondslave! Promise was that I
Should Israel from Philistian yoke deliver;
Ask for this great Deliverer now, and find him
Eyeless in Gaza at the Mill with slaves,
Himself in bonds under Philistian yoke.

ll. 36-42

Samson's concern is not the damage that his defeat has done to the name of God, nor even that Israel still groans under cruel foreign domination; he is concerned only with his personal humiliation in serving the Philistines as a slave. He is "debas't," he says, an indication of his damaged pride. The bitterness with which he says, "Ask for this great Deliverer now," is a particularly poignant innuendo that God has betrayed His "promise" in not allowing him to deliver Israel from the Philistines.

It is not that Samson in pitying his lot in life so intensely is ignorant of his irresponsibility. Briefly, he recognizes that perhaps he had some responsibility for his own incarceration. "What if all foretold / Had been fulfill'd but through mine own default," he asks; "Whom have I to complain of but myself?" (ll. 44-46). This is his first, tentative admission of guilt: it is possible that he, not God, is responsible for the fact that he has not yet delivered Israel from the Philistines. However, he soon relapses into self-pity, this time because of his blindness, and once again shifts the responsibility for his downfall off of his own shoulders. "Why am I thus bereav'd thy prime decree [of sight]?" he questions, indicating that he perceives Providence to have allowed his fall.

With the despair of the closing lines of his first speech, Samson falls into intense self-pity. He has, he says,

> a life half dead, a living death,
> And buried; but O yet more miserable!
> Myself my Sepulcher, a moving Grave,
> Buried, yet not exempt
> By privilege of death and burial
> From worst of other evils, pains and wrongs,
> But made hereby obnoxious more
> To all the miseries of life,
> Life in captivity
> Among inhuman foes.
>
> ll. 100-109

The oxymorons suggest the extremity of Samson's emotion and confusion. Because of his blindness and incarceration, he is "a living death" and "a moving grave." Unlike the dead, however, he is not exempt from suffering "evils, pains and wrongs," and from having to live life among "inhuman foes." The reader's first view of Samson's character is of a human being who is defeated, inwardly as well as outwardly. Yet this is the man whom Milton makes into a hero before the poem is over by giving him the experiences that develop a devotional attitude in him.

Manoa's visit early in the poem brings Samson face to face with his own pride. Manoa, Samson's father, counsels him to repent but not to demand punishment from God pridefully. His advice to Samson is that he should ask mercy, not justice, of God:

> Him who imploring mercy sues for life,
> Than who self-rigorous chooses death as due;
> Which argues over-just, and self-displeas'd
> For self- offence, more than for God offended.
>
> ll. 512-15

Manoa is clearly aware of his son's pride and he speaks in an effort to make Samson recognize his pride himself. It would be impious pride and presumption on Samson's part for him to take God's place by demanding a harsher punishment of himself than God demands.

Samson understands the implications of Manoa's argument perfectly, but he refuses to beg God for mercy. He is still proud. "His pardon I implore," Samson replies; "but as for life, / To what end should I seek it?" (ll. 521-22). Samson seems to consider his judgment regarding his life to be superior to God's. He laments that, even though he was gifted by God with superhuman strength and "all mortals [he] excell'd" (l. 532), he still fell to his pride and then into voluptuousness:

> Immeasurable strength they might behold
> In me, of wisdom nothing more than mean;
> This with the other should, at least, have pair'd,
> These two proportion'd ill drove me transverse.
>
> ll. 206-09

Had God given him the proportionate wisdom to handle his strength well, he argues, he would not have fallen. He accuses God of being remiss in not giving him wisdom equal to his physical strength. Clearly, Samson transfers blame to God and, therefore, avoids having to accept responsibility for himself; God's "disproportioned" gifts to Samson ruined him. This is "pride toward God," the first weakness that leads to Samson's defeat.

Not only does Samson blame God for his fall, but he also blames the leaders of the nation of Israel for not recognizing their deliverance at his hand. "That fault [Israel's continued enslavement to the Philistines], I take not on me," he states, "but transfer / On Israel's Governors" (ll. 241-42) who did not accept Samson's heroic exploits as God's method for their deliverance. Samson's condemnation of the leaders is both scathing and characteristic:

> Had Judah that day join'd, or one whole Tribe,
> They had by this possess'd the Towers of Gath.
> ll. 265-66

Had they taken the advantage which Samson afforded them, he argues, the Israelite governors could be free. But they chose "to love Bondage more than Liberty, / Bondage with ease than strenuous liberty" (ll. 271-72), Samson further laments. He himself chafes horribly under his bondage; he disdains those who choose servitude voluntarily.

Ironically, it is Manoa's criticism of God's providence that prompts Samson to rise above self-pity to true humility. Manoa says to Samson:

> Alas! methinks whom God hath chosen once
> To worthiest deeds, if he through frailty err,
> He should not so o'erwhelm, and as a thrall

Subject him to so foul indignities,
Be it but for honor's sake of former deeds.

ll. 368-72

As Samson's father, Manoa is sensitive to the injustice of his son's situation. Even if God does not respect Samson after he has fallen, Manoa thinks, He should at least honor his previous heroic deeds. That this statement prompts Samson's penitence is ironic because earlier in the poem Samson, as well as Manoa, had been critical of God's providence. Samson had taxed "divine disposal," as the chorus accused him (l. 210), when he lamented the fact that God had not given him wisdom adequate to handle his physical strength (ll. 206-09). In his conversation with Manoa, however, Samson acknowledges his own responsibility for his fall:

Appoint not heavenly disposition, Father,
Nothing of all these evils hath befall'n me
But justly; I myself have brought them on,
Sole Author I, sole cause: if aught seem vile,
As vile hath been my folly, who have profan'd
The mystery of God giv'n me under pledge
Of vow.

ll. 373-79a

He realizes that it was his own "profane," or unholy, attitude toward God's gifts of strength that caused his defeat, not God's malignity. For the first time in true humility, Samson acknowledges his "unworthiness in the sight of God" (CE, XVII, p. 65). It is when Samson sees himself as God sees him that he recognizes this unworthiness and submits himself before God.[5] Humility comes only as he focuses on God, not himself; when he thinks of his sinful attitude toward God, he loses his self-pity and pride. Furthermore, he realizes his fault in serving Dalila, not God, with his divinely-given strength. With this admission of failure, Samson finds his "former servitude" to Dalila "ignoble, / Unmanly, ignominious, infamous, / True slavery, and blindness worse than this, / That saw not how degenerately [he] serv'd" (ll. 416-19). When he realizes that he has debased his God-given strength to serve a woman, he admits his personal responsibility for his defeat and slavery.

Samson's marriage to Dalila points up his second weakness, namely his "impatience under the divine decrees" (CE, XVII, p. 69). No doubt sincerely eager to fulfill the divinely-appointed task of liberating Israel from the Philistines, Samson married Dalila, planning to use her to infiltrate the Philistines. Manoa, however, understands that there was more to Samson's motivation for marrying Dalila than a desire for Israel's liberty. He doubts Samson:

> I cannot praise thy marriage choices, Son,
> Rather approv'd them not; but thou didst plead
> Divine impulsion prompting how thou might'st
> Find some occasion to infest our Foes.
>
> ll. 420-23

Using the excuse that he was furthering his divine calling, Samson married Dalila in fact to satisfy his own lechery,[6] and, in so doing, "presumed" upon God's timing for the deliverance of his people.[7] Samson was impatient to fulfill his calling; he was unwilling to await God's time for His deliverance of the Israelites from Philistine bondage, and, therefore, used Dalila as a means to accomplish his task.

It is not Dalila, however, but Harapha who is the catalyst whereby Samson learns patience. Harapha ridicules Samson's pride as a warrior and calls his shame upon his head. Harapha shows insolence when he needles Samson with his claim, "To combat with a blind man I disdain, / And thou has need much washing to be toucht" (ll. 1106-07). Samson responds to Harapha's malicious taunt with amazing patience. He does not attack him, nor does he verbally lash out at him; he simply reminds Harapha of Dalila's treachery -- all the more heinous in Milton's narrative than in the biblical story because Milton makes Dalila Samson's wife.

Samson informs Harapha that his "trust is in the living God" (l. 1140) and then challenges him to man-to-man combat to prove which god, Dagon or Jehovah, is stronger. Though this is a simple statement on Samson's part, it is significant in that it shows some patience with God's providence. Samson begins to perceive of his conflict with Harapha as God's contest with Dagon. He "acquiesce[s] in the promises of God, through a confident reliance on his divine providence, power and goodness, and bear[s] inevitable evils with equanimity, as the dispensation of the Father, and sent for [his] good" (CE, XVII, p. 67). This is Milton's definition of devout patience in The Christian Doctrine. Because Samson has come to realize that "all the contest is now / Twixt God and Dagon" (ll. 461-62), not between Samson and Harapha, he can accept "inevitable evils with equanimity" and wait for God to vindicate Himself. Ironically, therefore, Harapha's visit begins to develop patience as a quality in Samson's character.

Samson's patience is not, however, perfect even after Harapha has tested it. Even though Samson acknowledges to Harapha that God has "inflicted" the "evils" of his present condition upon him "justly" (ll. 1169-71), he still relapses easily into the old impatient warrior. When Harapha calls him a "Murderer, a Revolter, and a Robber," Samson lashes back at him with "Tongue-doughty Giant, how dost thou prove me these?" (ll. 1180-81) Samson's pride surfaces again -- naturally enough. Milton does not remove Samson's pride at once; that would be psychologically unrealistic, given the extent to which pride ruled Samson's life before the action of the poem. Milton tests it again by Harapha's insults and thereby underscores his pride and impatience. John Spencer Hill is certainly correct when he says that Harapha does not teach Samson patience (p. 167) and cites Samson's following reaction to Harapha as evidence:

> Go baffl'd coward, lest I run upon thee,
> Though in these chains, bulk without spirit vast,
> And with one buffet lay thy structure low,

> Or swing thee in the Air, then dash thee down
> To the hazard of thy brains and shatter'd sides.
>
> ll. 1237-41

It is not Harapha who teaches Samson patience; it is Samson's increasing knowledge of himself that leads to patience. Harapha's insults are only the catalyst that helps Samson to understand how his pride and impatience have failed God in the past.

Just as Samson's humility is tested repeatedly throughout the poem, so to is his patience. Late in the poem, the Chorus provides Samson with the opportunity to prove his patience. Immediately before the officer comes to order Samson's presence at the feast to Dagon, the Chorus suggests to Samson that he will never be able to act on God's behalf again, but that he must remain quietly patient because of his blindness. The Chorus understands patience to mean the passivity with which some saints are called upon to endure the cruelty which the heathen inflict upon them; they expect that Samson will have to accept whatever ignominy the Philistines force upon him. But Samson has learned in his confrontation with Harapha that patience is an active "reliance" on God's help and plan, not passive suffering. His reply to the officer is simple, but apparently decisive: "I will not come" (l. 1342). Samson has the moral courage at this point to take an active stand for his God and await His disposition of the circumstances to His ends. Milton gives the concluding speech of the poem to the Chorus who notes that God's wisdom, not human wisdom, was best in Samson's case:

> All is best, though we oft doubt,
> What th'unsearchable dispose
> Of highest wisdom brings about.
>
> ll. 1745-47

Samson trusts God, and God vindicates him at the critical moment. Samson's newly-found patience provides him with the moral fortitude to turn a heathen feast into a divine rout.

Implicit in Samson's pride and impatience is his disobedience of God by not waiting for God's time for him to rescue Israel from the Philistines. In his initial soliloquy, Samson indicates a keen awareness of his failure as Israel's national deliverer. In shame, he laments:

> Why was my breeding order'd and prescrib'd
> As of a person separate to God,
> Design'd for great exploits; if I must die
> Betray'd, Captiv'd, and both my Eyes out,
> Made of my Enemies the scorn and gaze;
> To grind in Brazen Fetters under task
> With this Heav'n-gifted strength?
>
> ll. 30-36

Though these lines suggest a mild criticism of God's "betrayal" of him, Samson is also personally ashamed that he has disappointed God by his disobedience. Far from establishing "the will of God as the paramount rule of [his] conduct" (CE, XVII, p. 69) in his life before the action of the poem, Samson has chosen his own means of delivering Israel from foreign domination. The most important of these means, of course, is his marriage to Dalila which, we have already seen, was prompted by his own selfish desires as well as by his wish to free Israel from the Philistines. Samson's disobedience, therefore, is closely related to his impatience.[8]

Samson's disobedience is also related to his pride. When the Chorus reminds him that, for all of his physical prowess, Israel remains in captivity, Samson rejects the implicit blame somewhat high-handedly. He replies quickly, "That fault I take not on me, but transfer / On Israel's Governors" (ll. 241-42) who did not pursue the advantage which Samson's exploits had given them. Samson proudly disdains the Israelite leaders who loved "Bondage more than Liberty / Bondage with ease than strenuous liberty" (ll. 270-72). In pride, Samson takes matters into his own hands and kills several Philistines "singly" (l. 244). Essentially, Samson elevates his will over God's will. His impatience with Israel's leaders becomes disobedience of God; he fails to wait for God's appointed time for him to defeat Israel's enemy.

As Hill says of the Son in Paradise Regained, it is when Samson "will[s] to relax [his] will" in favor of God's will that he learns obedience. The deliberate choice to subordinate the human will to the divine is, to quote Hill again, a "spiritual state which is the apex of self-knowledge and the apotheosis of human potential" (p. 183). Samson's development toward this spiritual state of submission to God is the action of the poem. As William G. Riggs states in The Christian Poet in "Paradise Lost", "In contemplation of his own acts and potential for action, the Miltonic hero [Samson, in this case] discovers God in himself. Through temptation he is perfected in obedience and rectitude" (p. 188). Samson is given the opportunity to obey God when the public officer comes to command his attendance at the feast to Dagon.

Samson is in a dilemma when he is commanded to appear at the Philistine feast. For him to attend would be a blasphemous contravention of his Nazarite vow:

> Thou knowst I am an Ebrew, therefore tell them
> Our Law forbids at thir Religious Rites
> My presence; for that cause I cannot come.
> ll. 1319-21

Samson refuses to go to the celebration three times. His refusals to "prostitute holy things to Idols" (l. 1358) demonstrate a returning moral fortitude and strength of character which he lacked as late as his challenge to Harapha to physical combat. Here, at least, Samson "stand[s] still" on his own moral integrity;[9] he acts on what he perceives God's will to be at the time.

There is an important irony in Samson's final decision to go to the feast for Dagon after he has refused earlier to go. This decision is the climax of Samson's experience of devotion to God in the poem. He states his reason for going to be "some rousing motions" of divine inspiration:

> I begin to feel
> Some rousing motions in me which dispose
> To something extraordinary my thoughts.
> I with this Messenger will go along,
> Nothing to do, be sure, that may dishonor
> Our Law, or stain my vow of Nazarite.
>   ll. 1381-86

This is the only instance in the poem of Samson's claiming inspiration for an action that he is about to undertake.[10] In Toward "Samson Agonistes", Mary Ann Radzinowicz notes that the irony of Samson's decision to go to Dagon's feast is that he is doing so in obedience to God. She explains that Samson "no longer obey[s] the law; [he obeys] the spirit" (p. 261). By determining to obey divine promptings when they come to him, then, Samson rises above his own preconceived notions of obedience to a literal law into a more immediate experience of God's direction in his life. His decision to go to the Philistine feast, which, he assures the Chorus, will not involve disobedience of any moral strictures of the law (ll. 1407-09), is devout obedience. He undertakes this task in direct obedience to the "rousing motions" in him. It is, to quote Radzinowicz again, a "deed of faith; its value [lies] in his understanding of his God and his willing not of his own death but of God's glory" (p. 263). Samson exercises an active choice to obey God at His time, not his own.

Milton is careful in his presentation of Samson's decision to obey the "rousing motions" of God in his soul to go to the feast. He wishes us to be sure that Samson is not compelled by God to go -- after all, Samson had disobeyed God before and found himself blind and in prison as a result. Samson is not God's puppet. He goes willingly, paradoxically manifesting a "true experience" (l. 1756) of devotion to God. Samson explains his free choice to the Chorus:

> Where outward force constrains, the sentence holds;
> But who constrains me to the Temple of Dagon,
> Not dragging? The Philistian Lords command.
> Commands are no constraints. If I obey them,
> I do it freely; venturing to displease
> God for the fear of Man, and Man prefer,
> Set God behind: which in his jealousy
> Shall never, unrepented, find forgiveness.
> Yet that he may dispense with me or thee
> Present in Temples at Idolatrous Rites
> For some important cause, thou needst not doubt.
>> ll. 1369-79

Deliberately choosing God over man, Samson goes to the feast "freely" and thereby demonstrates his mature devotion in obedience to God's immediate promptings in his soul.

Samson's last weakness to be transformed into devotion for God rather than pity for self is his despair. In "The Idea as Pattern: Despair and Samson Agonistes," Don Cameron Allen argues that despair is Samson's primary flaw. Allen's argument focuses primarily on the "theological dicta on the genesis and cure of despair" (p. 53) which were contemporaneous with Milton. I wish, however, to pay attention to the poet's modulation of Samson's despair, through doubt, and finally into hope in devotional terms, not "theological dicta."

Samson betrays his despair in his first speech. Lamenting his blindness, he calls out:

> O dark, dark, dark, amid the blaze of noon,
> Irrecoverably dark, total Eclipse
> Without all hope of day!
> O first created Beam, and thou great Word,
> "Let there be light, and light was over all";
> Why am I thus bereav'd thy prime decree?
>
> ll. 80-86

There is, of course, no hope that he will ever see light again; everything is "irrecoverably dark . . . / Without all hope of day!" Milton's choice of blindness as a symbol of despair is fitting, not only because he himself knew of its agonies, but because it is final; there is no hope for the blind to see. Milton writes of despair in The Christian Doctrine, stating that it "takes place only in the reprobate" (CE, XVII, p. 59). In Milton's view, regenerate men do not experience despair. It casts men beyond God's help. Milton cites Cain as an example of despair: cast off by God forever, Cain laments, "My punishment is greater than I can bear" (Genesis 4:13). To demonstrate the extremity of his own despair, Samson describes himself as living

> a life half dead, a living death,
> And buried; but O yet more miserable!
> Myself my Sepulcher, a moving Grave.
>
> ll. 100-102

In this speech, the oxymorons such as "living death" betray the despair he feels, completely "dead" to hope of recovery.

In response to Manoa's reproach that he has brought "dishonor" to God (ll. 433-47), Samson begins to take his first tentative steps toward hope. He understands that God will vindicate His name; "all the contest is now / 'Twixt God and Dagon," he says, and God "will arise and his great name assert" (ll. 461-62; 467). He is confident that God will not be defeated by Dagon, but he doubts that he will ever be God's instrument to rout Dagon. He regards himself at this point to be "overthrown" (l. 463), defeated, and of no further use to God. The conversation with Manoa marks a movement from despair to doubt in Samson's mind. He no longer despairs that all is lost for God; he merely doubts his future effectiveness for God's work. As Milton states in The Christian Doctrine, "even the pious [the regenerate] are liable, at least for a time" to doubt (CE, XVII, p. 59). Manoa's indictment of Samson, then, allows Samson to move from despair to doubt.

Ironically, Harapha is the one who brings Samson to hope in God. Harapha attacks Samson with the same doubt that Samson earlier experienced, the fear that God has turned His back on him. Harapha drives home his attack with every phrase in this speech:

> Presume not on thy God, whate'er he be,
> Thee he regards not, owns not, hath cut off
> Quite from his people, and delivered up
> Into thy Enemies' hand.
>
> ll. 1156-59

This is the worst solitude of all for Samson, cut off not only from his people, but from God. However, Harapha is not aware, as we are, that already Samson has begun to move beyond his earlier despair and doubt.

Samson's reply to Harapha's taunt is lucid and hopeful:

> All these indignities, for such they are
> From thine, these evils I deserve and more,
> Acknowledge them from God inflicted on me
> Justly, yet despair not of his final pardon
> Whose ear is ever open; and his eye
> Gracious to re-admit the suppliant;
> In confidence whereof I once again

> Defy thee to the trial of mortal fight,
> By combat to decide whose god is God,
> Thine or whom I with Israel's Sons adore.
>
> ll. 1168-77

In this speech, Samson foreshadows his victory at the end of the poem. He grants Harapha that he "deserves" all of the "evils" which the Philistine has enumerated, yet he demonstrates a perspective on his situation that Harapha cannot understand. Samson hopes for God's "pardon," not His justice. God's "ear is ever open," Samson asserts, "and his eye / Gracious to re-admit the suppliant." Even though he deserves punishment, Samson realizes that his God is merciful, too. Samson's statement is significant because it demonstrates that his devotional experience is maturing: now it is God, not himself, who is the focus of his self analysis. He realizes that his God is greater than his sin --not because He punishes sin, but because He forgives it and "re-admits the suppliant" to His grace. As Galbraith M. Crump says, Samson comes to "define himself" in a theocentric universe" (p.3). Don Cameron Allen interprets Samson's speech to be a microcosm of the climax of the whole poem:

> With this speech we know that Samson will not die an apathetic death. Life has returned to him; and though he does not yet know how it will all be brought about, he is God's champion once more. There is no temptation in this scene and no comedy; it is the most important scene of all, for it is the hinge of the tragedy. By the victory over Harapha, who symbolizes all that is valiant in Philistia, God, working through Samson, has put Dagon down. It is, in truth, the final event of the tragedy in miniature.
>
> p. 61

Harapha's goading, therefore, results in Samson's first statement of hope in God's mercy. This development in Samson's character is important because he needs hope when he decides to obey God and go to the Philistine feast.

In addition to the obedience which he demonstrates so clearly when he defends his decision to go to Dagon's temple, Samson goes to perform his final act on God's behalf with hope as well. He informs the Chorus that the "rousing motions" which prompt him to go to the celebration "dispose" his thoughts "to something extraordinary" (ll. 1382-83). He is somewhat enigmatic in that he does not explain what extraordinary thoughts he has. "This day," he says again to the Chorus, "will be remarkable in my life / By some great act, or of my days the last" (ll. 1388-89). Without providing any specific detail for the Chorus, Samson intimates that he has great events in mind. What the Chorus does not know, however, the reader does. We know that Samson will pull the temple down in one last "act of conquest" (as Barbara Lewalski says of the Son in <u>Paradise Regained</u>);[11] therefore, we can understand Samson's feeling of hope at this point in the dramatic action. He has lamented God's apparent desertion of him; at the climax of the poem, however, "some rousing motions" reassure him that God has more for him to do. In fact, Samson hopes that God will fulfill His promise to him that He would use him to deliver the Israelites from the Philistines. This is devout hope as Milton defines it in <u>The Christian Doctrine</u>: there is no room for despair, or even doubt, in hope; there is room only for a certain expectation that God will fulfill His promises -- His specific promises.

Samson is Milton's everyman. He is fallen; therefore, he lacks the innocent, spontaneous experience of devotion which the prelapsarian Adam and Eve have in <u>Paradise Lost</u>. He is defeated; therefore, he does not earn the right, as the Son does in <u>Paradise Regained</u>, to be an example of the right experience of devotion. However, more than Adam, and even more than the Son, Samson is alone with his God. Adam's sin necessitates mature devotion for spiritual growth to occur; the Son in obedience guarantees devotion to fallen men; Samson experiences devotion which helps him to know himself because he comes to know

God. He is no longer in need of devotion as are Adam and Eve; he is certainly not an examplar of devotion as is the Son; he practices devotion.

Notes
Chapter Five

[1]Hill disagrees on p. 153, stating that Samson "is not an ordinary man; he is a Judge, an Israelite shophet elect above the rest of mankind."

[2]Galbraith M. Crump, "Introduction," in Twentieth Century Interpretations of "Samson Agonistes", ed. G.M. Crump (Englewood Cliffs, New Jersey: Prentice Hall, Inc., 1968), p. 3.

[3]Balachandra Rajan, The Lofty Rhyme: A Study of Milton's Major Poetry (Coral Gables, Florida: University of Miami Press, 1970), p. 133.

[4]William G. Madsen, "From Shadowy Types to Truth," in Twentieth Century Interpretations of "Samson Agonistes", ed. G.M. Crump (Englewood Cliffs, New Jersey: Prentice Hall, Inc., 1968), p. 95. Madsen agrees with Rajan in this regard.
All subsequent references to secondary materials on Samson Agonistes are to this volume, unless otherwise noted.

[5]Hill, p. 159.

[6]Allen, "The Idea as Pattern: Despair and Samson Agonistes," in Twentieth Century Interpretations of "Samson Agonistes", p. 59.

[7]Hill, p. 158.

[8]cf. Allen, p. 51.

[9]Rajan, p. 129.

[10]Manoa claims that Samson argued "divine impulsion for his marriage choices" (ll. 421-23).

[11]Barbara Lewalski, "Theme and Action in Paradise Regained," p. 344.

Conclusion

Milton writes, and his poetic characters live, "within the vast dimensions of a theocentric universe."[1] For Milton as a poet, the omnipresence of God means that he must "assert Eternal Providence" to men and also express his own unforced love to God. There is, therefore, an important tension in Milton's poems which results from their being simultaneously theodicies and devotions: how does a poet explain God's ways to men while insisting that men are free to accept or reject divine providence? The answer lies in the devotional experiences of Milton's poet-speakers and poetic characters who "will to relax [their] will[s]."[2] Paradoxically, the development of self-knowledge for Milton's characters results from knowing God.

As he looks back on his life from 1642 in The Reason of Church Government, Milton makes it clear that he deliberately chose to write poetry and that he had specific purposes in mind when he determined to write. "I assent[ed]," he writes,

> to an inward prompting which now grew daily upon me. That by labor and intent study. . . joined with the strong propensity of nature, I might perhaps leave something so written to aftertimes, as they should not willingly let it die. These thoughts at once possessed me . . . [that] there ought no regard be sooner had than to God's glory. . . . For which cause, . . . I applied myself to that resolution . . . to fix all the industry and art I could unite to the adorning of my native tongue; not to make verbal curiosities the end, that were a

toilsome vanity, but to be an interpreter and relater of the
best and sagest things among mine own citizens throughout
this island in the mother dialect. That what the greatest and
choicest wits of Athens, Rome or modern Italy, and those
Hebrews of old did for their country, I, in my proportion, with
this over and above of being a Christian, might do for mine.

p. 668

Personally inclined, by "an inward prompting," to write poetry, Milton
studied to become a poet. He indicates that he had two purposes in mind
when he made this decision: he wished to raise the English language, his
"mother dialect," to a high level by writing of the "best and sagest things";
and, second, "being a Christian," he wished to write for "God's glory."
There is no reason to doubt that Milton's poetry reflects these purposes.

The poetry that Milton is thinking of in The Reason of Church
Government is, in part, the poems written between 1629 and 1637 which
the second chapter of this study considers. In those poems, Milton
develops his poetic talents until, in "Lycidas," he writes one of the finest
pastoral elegies in the English language. These years are private,
preparatory years, a "melic period," as Don Cameron Allen terms it in The
Harmonious Vision (p. 56), though Edward King's death is an intrusion of
the real world with its suffering and death. "Lycidas," Milton's elegy for
King, is not only a fine pastoral elegy, however; it is also a perfectly-
controlled devotion.

In the "Nativity Ode," written to celebrate Christmas in 1629, Milton
establishes a pattern of devotion which becomes useful for him in
"Lycidas." The "Nativity Ode" celebrates God's love in sending the "Heav'n-
born child" (l. 30) to redeem men from their sins. As an act of devotion, the
poem celebrates hope. Reflecting upon the incarnation of Christ and
seeking to write a "humble ode" (l. 24) to adore the infant, the speaker
places himself in the position of an eyewitness to the nativity. By
"observing" the nativity, the speaker experiences the fulfillment of God's

Old Testament prophecies that He would send a Savior. Because of the trust in God's promises which the incarnation gives him, he confidently projects the Savior's death at Calvary "our great redemption from above" to bring (l. 4). It is this projected hope for redemption that makes the speaker's experience in the poem devotional.

"Lycidas" is clearly an act of devotion. Its subject, however, is not religious; its subject is death, a painful reminder of sin and evil. Just as Bethlehem guaranteed Calvary for the speaker in the "Nativity Ode," so too Lycidas' resurrection assures the speaker's resurrection. Devotion is perhaps most difficult in the face of death, for death seems to undo all that God as creator has done. But as the speaker in "Lycidas" moves through a complex series of classical and Christian materials, trying to assuage his grief, he finally focuses on the hope of a personal resurrection predicated on "the dear might of him that walk'd the waves" (l. 173). As a result of facing death, then, not in spite of the presence of death, the speaker experiences a mature hope in a personal resurrection which is guaranteed in the poem by Lycidas' immortality. "Lycidas" is, therefore, a self-contained devotion which celebrates hope in God's victory over death.

It is death -- and its cause, sin[3] -- that matures the devotional experience of Adam and Eve in <u>Paradise Lost</u>. Created in innocence and able to enjoy all that God bestows upon them, Adam and Eve experience love for God and gratitude to Him. But God gave them a free will and thereby demanded that their obedience to Him be freely given. In effect, Adam and Eve's obedience to God's command to cultivate the garden and not to eat of the tree of the knowledge of good and evil is their expression of devotion to God. Because they are free to disobey, their obedience is an active choice on their parts. When they disobey God in Book Nine, however, they risk losing their devotional experience of God altogether -- for the only result of disobedience they have been taught is death. However, God by His grace offers forgiveness and a "second chance" to Adam and Eve and "His Spirit within them" a "paradise within" (XII, ll. 488 and 587). Rather than destroying devotion, therefore, sin results in Adam and Eve maturing in their expression of devotion to God: whereas, before the fall, they worshipped God only as their creator and provider, after the fall they worship Him as their redeemer as well. Adam and Eve learn humility, patience and hope in Paradise Lost, all predicated on God's love for them after they have fallen. Just as Milton develops a justification for God's ways to men in Paradise Lost, so too he expands the devotional experience of the poem's human protagonists in response to God's mercy.

Whereas the "first Adam" sins in Paradise Lost and is restored by God's grace, the "second Adam" -- the Son in Paradise Regained -- remains obedient to the Father and thereby earns the right to redeem fallen men. By emphasizing the Son's humanity in Paradise Regained, Milton is able to develop his character in the poem. As man, the Son learns patience and obedience to the Father in the face of Satan's temptations. He "achieve[s] self-knowledge," Mary Ann Radzinowicz states in Toward "Samson Agonistes", "in relation to a conception of God, and [by acting] in conformity to that knowledge" (p. 246). The Son comes to understand himself only in relation to the Father. Because he remains obedient throughout the poem to the Father's calling, he himself develops in his character as a man. The Son not only earns a "fairer Paradise" (IV, l. 613) for the sons of men, he also experiences that paradise himself. Mary Ann Radzinowicz writes, "The Son gives grace to man to live under the guidance of the pattern of behavior which produced that grace" (p. 250). The Son is both the agent of redemption and the model of the redeemed man. He is both because, as John Spencer Hill writes in John Milton: Poet, Priest and Prophet, he "[assists] divine disposal [the call to redeem men] by his own responsive choices" (p. 179).

In Samson Agonistes, Milton puts devotion to work in the service of God. Though restored by the end of Paradise Lost, Adam and Eve leave the garden of Eden with "The World . . . all before them" (XII, l. 646). They do not serve God after their fall in any active manner analogous to their cultivation of the garden before the fall. Though the Son in Paradise Regained is "genuinely subject to temptation [and] able to fall,"[4] he remains sinless. Therefore, his service for God is uninterrupted. Samson, however, falls, is forgiven, and finally restored to active service for God.

Samson's sins are legion: he is proud of his physical strength; he is impatient with God's apparent delay in delivering Israel; he is disobedient to his Nazarite vow in marrying Dalila; and he is in doubt, even despair, when the action of the poem begins. Samson is not, however, separated from God. Though Milton brings no supernatural visitors to Samson, only the Jews and the Philistines, Samson is always conscious of God's hand in his life. Indeed, Samson is alone with God even when others are there in the prison with him; the action of the poem is internal, that is, in the spiritual development of the protagonist.

Samson does not "pay" for his sins in the poem; he has already paid a terrible price for his sins before the poem begins. Rather, he is forgiven of his sins and learns how to turn them into active expressions of devotion to God. For his pride in his ability to rescue Israel by his strength alone, he learns the humility that he is the "Sole Author" (l. 377) of his own defeat and humiliation. For his impatience in hurrying God's plans by marrying Dalila, he learns to have patience; in the face of Harapha's derision, Samson grants that "all the contest is now / 'Twixt God and Dagon (ll. 461-62), not his own. For disobedience to God, Samson learns to obey God's "rousing motions" (l. 1382) and to go to the feast, though he would not go when he was first commanded to do so. For the despair that God had cast him off forever, Samson learns the hope that God will use him in His service yet one more time. In sum, the meaning of Samson's life is "to grow toward knowledge of God" and then to put the "more profound faith" that he learns into service for God.[5]

Though Milton presents God's actions in men's lives in his poems, he writes from the human as well as the divine perspective. The poems are not versified theological treatises. They are expressions of fallen man's struggle to know God and to love Him. Milton certainly justifies God in his poems, but he does so by clothing the "Word" with "flesh" -- by re-creating "paradise" in the experiences of his characters. The angels' praise of the

Son at the conclusion of <u>Paradise Regained</u> applies to all of Milton's protagonists. Each one gains the "True Image of the Father . . . enshrine'd / In fleshly Tabernacle and human form" (IV, ll. 596-99).

Notes
Conclusion

[1]Galbraith M. Crump, "Introduction," in <u>Twentieth Century Interpretations of "Samson Agonistes"</u>, ed. G.M. Crump (Englewood Cliffs, New Jersey: Prentice Hall, Inc., 1968), p. 3.

[2]Hill, p. 183.

[3]cf. Romans 6:23. "For the wages of sin is death."

[4]Barbara Lewalski, "Theme and Action in <u>Paradise Regained</u>," in <u>Milton's Epic Poetry: Essays on "Paradise Lost" and "Paradise Regained"</u>, ed. C. A. Patrides (Harmondsworth, England: Penguin Books, 1967), p. 323.

[5]Radzinowicz, p. 250.

Bibliography

Allen, Don Cameron. <u>The Harmonious Vision: Studies in Milton's Poetry</u>. Baltimore: Johns Hopkins Press, 1954.

Barker, Arthur. "The Pattern of Milton's 'Nativity Ode'." <u>University of Toronto Quarterly</u>, X (1941), 167-81.

Bush, Douglas. <u>John Milton: A Sketch of His Life and Writings</u>. New York: Collier Books, 1964.

Crump, Galbraith M., ed. <u>Twentieth Century Interpretations of "Samson Agonistes"</u>. Englewood Cliffs, New Jersey: Prentice Hall Inc., 1968.

Drabble, Margaret, ed. <u>The Oxford Companion to English Literature</u> 5th ed. (Oxford: Clarendon Press, 1986), p. 1140.

Evans, J.M. <u>"Paradise Lost" and the Genesis Tradition</u>. New York: Oxford University Press, 1968.

Hanford, James Holly. <u>A Milton Handbook</u>. 4th ed. New York: Appleton-Century-Crofts Inc., 1946.

----------. "That Shepherd Who First Taught the Chosen Seed." <u>University of Toronto Quarterly</u>, VII (1939), pp. 403-409.

Hazelton, Roger. "The Devotional Life." In <u>A Companion to the Study of St. Augustine</u>. Ed. Roy Battenhouse. New York: Oxford University Press, 1969, pp. 399-416.

Hill, John Spencer. <u>John Milton: Poet, Priest and Prophet</u>. Totowa, New Jersey: Rowman and Littlefield, 1979.

Hollander, John. <u>The Untuning of the Sky: Ideas of Music in English Poetry, 1500-1700</u>. Princeton: Princeton University Press, 1961.

Holloway, John. "<u>Paradise Lost</u> and the Quest for Reality." <u>Forum for Modern Language Studies</u>, III (1967), pp. 1-14.

Hughes, Merritt Y., ed. <u>John Milton: Complete Poems and Major Prose</u>. New York: The Odyssey Press, 1957.

Kelley, Maurice. This Great Argument: A Study of Milton's "De Doctrina Christiana" as a Gloss upon "Paradise Lost." Princeton: Princeton University Press, 1941.

Lewalski, Barbara. Protestant Poetics and the Seventeenth Century Religious Lyric. Princeton: Princeton University Press, 1979.

----------. "Theme and Action in Paradise Regained." In Milton's Epic Poetry: Essays on "Paradise Lost" and "Paradise Regained". Harmondsworth, England: Penguin Books, 1967, pp. 322-47.

Martz, Louis L. The Meditative Poem. New York: New York University Press, 1963.

----------. The Paradise Within: Studies in Vaughan, Traherne, and Milton. New Haven: Yale University Press, 1964.

----------. The Poetry of Meditation. New Haven: Yale University Press, 1954.

Patrides, C.A., ed. Milton's "Lycidas": The Tradition and the Poem. New York: Holt, Rinehart, Winston, 1961.

Patterson, Frank Allen, ed. The Works of John Milton. 20 vols. New York: Columbia University Press, 1931-42.

Radzinowicz, Mary Ann. Toward "Samson Agonistes": The Growth of Milton's Mind. Princeton: Princeton University Press, 1978.

Rajan, Balachandra. The Lofty Rhyme: A Study of Milton's Major Poetry. Coral Gables, Florida: University of Miami Press, 1970.

Riggs, William G. The Christian Poet in "Paradise Lost". Berkeley: University of California Press, 1972.

Rivers, Isabel. Classical and Christian Ideas in English Renaissance Poetry. Boston: George Allen and Unwin, 1979.

Rosenberg, Donald M. Oaten Reeds and Trumpets: Pastoral and Epic in Virgil, Spenser and Milton. East Brunswick, New Jersey: Bucknell University Press, 1981.

Saurat, Denis. Milton: Man and Thinker. New York: The Dial Press, Inc., 1925.

Sewell, Arthur. A Study in Milton's Christian Doctrine. Folcroft, PA: Archon Books, 1967.

Summers, Joseph H. The Muse's Method. Cambridge: Harvard University Press, 1962.

157

Tillyard, E.M.W. <u>Studies in Milton</u>. London: Chatto and Windus, 1951.

Tuve, Rosemond. <u>Images and Themes in Five Poems by Milton</u>. Cambridge: Harvard University Press, 1957.

Woodhouse, A.S.P. <u>The Poet and His Faith: Religion and Poetry in England from Spenser to Eliot and Dryden</u>. Chicago: University of Chicago Press, 1965.

----------. "Theme and Pattern in <u>Pattern Regained</u>." <u>University of Toronto Quarterly</u>, XXV (1955-56), p. 181.

Index

STUDIES IN ART AND RELIGIOUS INTERPRETATION